This book is designed to provide information and positive motivation to readers. It is sold with the understanding that the author is not engaged to render any type of psychological, legal, or any other kind of professional advice. The content of this book is the sole expression and opinion of its author. No warranties or guarantees are expressed or implied by the author's choice to include any of the content in this volume.

www.timsmarshall.com

Printed in the United States of America
First Edition: February 2018

TABLE OF CONTENTS

TABLE OF CONTENTS

TABLE OF CONTENTS

TABLE OF CONTENTS

TABLE OF CONTENTS

TABLE OF CONTENTS

TABLE OF CONTENTS

PROLOGUE

"Success is achieved by starting something that you intended to do, and continuously acting upon your intentions."

—Tim Marshall

"The absolute power created when you break through your fears will change your life forever."

—Tim Marshall

I AM RESPONSIBLE FOR MY OWN HAPPINESS. NO ONE ELSE IS.

Life is made of billions of moments linked together. Each moment is important. Once a moment passes you can never recapture it. The moments of your life pile together to form your world, good or bad. What if you took each moment and wrung the beauty and potential from it? Imagine this life.

But how do you know what potential lies in the moment? Through fear and indecision, and perhaps laziness, we let these moments slip away. And soon these lost moments pile up to become your current situation. But worse, as the new current moments pile up, they become future moments. Now you are truly lost in potential.

Look at your life and surroundings as a beautiful miniature glass globe. Is it the globe that you dreamed of creating? If you shook it, would all of the figures stay upright or would everything fall over into a heap of disarray? You build this globe.

No one else. And no matter what you think now, you have the ability to create the beautiful globe you desire. And I will help you get there.

WHAT YOU NEED

First, you will need an open mind. Otherwise, both you and I are wasting our time. If you aren't open to absorbing my philosophy of life success, what is the point of me presenting it to you? This will become just another pile of wasted moments.

Part of an open mind is awareness. In fact, it is not part, it is a huge critical piece. But most of us are so involved within ourselves that we are not aware of the true reality around us. We filter everything through our self-perception, looking outward, rather than stepping outside of ourselves and looking at the glass globe.

An open mind and awareness will unleash in you an entirely new vision of your world.

It will reveal opportunities that you see, act upon, and finalize.

DOING WHAT YOU FEAR

Fear is a horrible emotion in life. It keeps us chained to a limited existence. Think about this: Our fears, most self-created through incorrect self-analysis, start to rule our actions. What does this cause? It cripples our ability to move forward and to reach our potential. We become rooted in the fears created in our past moments. This creates paralysis. We literally cripple ourselves and our potential. If you lose a leg, you have a physical limitation that will prevent you from playing football. We all realize this. But if you hold a fear, you have the exact same emotional and mental result: you're stopped from doing what you want. But unlike the physical barrier, in this case you can learn to overcome it.

It takes an open mind and awareness. You first have to become aware of the fear, then you have to analyze the fear, then you have to determine the legitimacy of the fear. Often, it was one bad experience in life that created this fear. But we inflate this episode into a life-defining barrier, rather than chipping away at it.

By embracing the approach in this book, you will surge into optimism, confidence, accomplishment and most importantly, peace of mind.

By breaking through your wall of closed-minded perceptions and fears, you will be able to peel back the thin or thick layer of protection (your safety zone) which is paralyzing you. This will free you to develop the uniqueness that is you, and to truly realize your potential in *all areas* of your life.

IT DOESN'T MATTER WHERE YOU ARE NOW

It does not matter where you are currently in your life personally, professionally or financially.

Once you realize the three pillars of an open mind, awareness, and fear, and act upon them, your life will change. And quite dramatically.

You will move outside of your comfort zone. You will become excited at small victories. You will realize the potential ahead. You will be living in the present moment as opposed to yesterday's stagnant comfort zone.

CHALLENGES

Challenges bring excitement and awareness to the moment. Once you identify an old restrictive perception, you have the ability to make a choice to open the door to a new thought, behavior or experience. Your positive actions will energize your senses towards the creation and enthusiasm of exploring something new. Your old, "they achieved success because they had the success gene or luck," becomes "I will achieve success. Why not me?"

GROWING A LEGACY

"As we look ahead into the next century, leaders will be those who empower others."* — *Bill Gates

One of the greatest contributions you can make is creating a legacy that helps others.

Your own good actions and positive life will lead others to want to become better themselves. Small successes add up. And each time you will be adding a figure to your glass globe. These pieces will start to accumulate.

Many of us have left this world with our globes unfinished. But it doesn't have to be this way. Your life, and the creation of your globe, is in your hands. You have control over creating this legacy. Don't hesitate. The moments are streaking by.

ASK YOURSELF

- What is our desired image of yourself?
- Do you see this image as something you can achieve?
- Do you believe in yourself?
- Do you fear the unknown?
- Do you protect yourself with a closed mind?
- Have you given yourself a permanent label?
- What legacy do you want to create?

Limiting our behaviors sabotages our relationships, success, and life. Self-defeating behaviors do not exist randomly, and they are not permanent. You can change them. And we will in the pages of this book.

MENTAL LIFESTYLE

Do you have an open mind? Test yourself: Do you wish people were more like you? Or do you wish you were more like other people? Do you judge who they are? Or do you think they judge you? Do you say to yourself, "if only they would do this?" Or, "if they only knew who I really am?" Does fear of change terrify you? Do you feel stuck in a job or relationship? Do you hide from the reality of your financial situation? Or if you have wealth, does your financial situation dictate a life that you don't particularly want to live? If you answered "yes" to any of these questions, we have work to do.

HOW TO READ THIS BOOK

More than 90 percent of the information we learn does not stick with us because we are caught up in our cemented thoughts. We can read, listen to informational CDs, attend presentations and meetings and forget everything almost immediately or, over a couple of weeks it dissipates and we go right back to our comfort zone. Another way of stating it is that we stay in our fear zone.

So, Strategy One: When reading this book, highlight the teaching points and write out bullet points with your own interpretation of them.

Interact with the book so it becomes part of you.

Strategy Two: Put into *daily practice* what you learn. You have the gift of choice of actions, but you have to start using those choices.

This book is a systematic journey of continuous practice steps that lower the bars of being stuck in our current thoughts, of being fearful and close-minded. The reason why new information does not stick is because we defensively reel in our old theater play, out of fear, and this overrides the potential of the new play. Hence, little is learned or gained, and status quo prevails.

If you want consistent personal accomplishments, growth, and financial freedom, you have to open yourself up to new ways and ideas.

My accomplishments in sales, management, leadership, speaking, teaching, ownership and friendship/relationships are all based on this principle: Have an open mind, practice awareness and do what I fear to do. Acceptance of these words has ended my complacency and second-guessing.

My abilities increase the more I practice and do what I fear. What I thought was a challenge becomes a victory. Confidence replaces fear.

You may not know who I am, but by the time you finish this book, you will.

I will replace some of the old fluff of personal development thinking with my "real life" relentless action techniques, with powerful and permanent practice systems that you can incorporate into your life. This will lead to amazing small and large victories and create the willingness to embrace the challenges that come with momentum.

I truly understand the struggles of our deepest pains and obstacles because I lived in them, fought them, and conquered them.

I will not have a long list of items to challenge you, or a list that will last for weeks. I will have real-life examples and practice techniques that will impact you immediately and positively. But, you will have to make decisions. A decision that is based on changing behavior is only a decision if you practice supporting your decision until you become that decision. You have to be redundant and never give up practicing, otherwise your decision will be a hope that never grows into a new way of living.

Let's start our first practice. Get used to saying your name and get used to hearing my name, Tim Marshall. That is our identity. Cherish it. That is our first building block together.

Embracing your name can be your starting point to changing your life and embracing your uniqueness.

Donald Trump is an expert at this. You might not agree with him, but he is a master at marketing his name, and he does this fearlessly. The same goes for Oprah. She has created a dynasty with her name, backed up by relentless positive action. Practice associating a strong image with your name. No one in the world is the same as you. No one.

Live your name and love it!

As far as the content of this book, you'll find material that is new and unique. You will find philosophies that have been simplified for everyday use. All of it is important.

Open yourself up and grow in your unique shoes. We all are so unique and there is not one other person out there that is the same as you. You are the greatest model. You just need to build the greatest engine inside that model, and build it the way you want, with your powerful name behind it.

A STREAMLINED APPROACH

1. You are the decision maker on how you want to think and act. There is no finger pointing if you are 18 or older; you have complete control over your decisions and your life. Your past is your past, and how you live now is your greatest opportunity ever!

2. If you are not open to greatness, then someone else will be. Look around you. Someone is achieving amazing results. Why not you?

3. If you are open and you show interest, you will have a line of people waiting to meet you.

4. Your actions will start the process.

5. Your "bullseye" is what drives you. We will examine this in the book.

6. Retention of information is only useful if you are open to practicing it. We can read and read and wish and wish, but if you don't practice what you learn, then you will become a turtle.

7. There are only moments. And when a moment is lost, you do not regain it. What you do with the moments pile up to create your actions.

8. Good actions create good thoughts and the reverse holds true.

9. Opening your mind builds internal and external wealth.

10. Lastly, formulate your own playbook. This book is a guide and a bible. But you must do your own research. We can't do that for you. We will provide the blueprint, but you must build the house.

#1

AWARENESS TAKES YOU BEHIND CLOSED DOORS

You can't accomplish anything without awareness. And I am not talking lip service to awareness.

If you see the word "awareness" in this book, *take notice.*

It is critical.

You have to dig into yourself and your surroundings. You must force yourself to be aware of your true past, your true present, your true behavior and its results, and your true thoughts. Who are you? No spin zone here. You have to sit down and analyze your life thoroughly to become truly aware of what is going on inside of you and outside of you.

WHAT IS YOUR DEFINITION OF BEING AWARE?

Being aware is identifying what hurts, holds you back due to fear, or drags you down with self-defeating thoughts.

These cripple freedom in your current moments, which in turn will limit your future actions.

Lack of awareness leads you to an eggshell existence. What you think you perceive is covered up by a thin layer of self-defense that your mind provides to protect you. Without awareness, you never see true reality until someone or something cracks your eggshell. It is decidedly better to crack your own eggshell than to have outside forces do it.

"The first step toward change is awareness.
The second step toward change is acceptance."
—Nathaniel Branden

IMPORTANT AWARENESS POINTS

- We see the world through our own narrow view. We resist change and find ease in what is familiar. We don't want to rock the boat with awareness. If you lack self-awareness, you will struggle to understand your strengths and weaknesses. The pure fact of not being aware can lead to the loss of financial security, relationships, opportunities and personal growth.

- **One of the worst things you can do . . . Not being honest with yourself.**

- You are the only person who knows the truth within yourself. If you are not honest with yourself, then you are sending mixed messages of who you really are. You are choosing not to be aware. We can convince ourselves of distorted realities to justify what we want to think, versus the reality of the situation. Feeding yourself half-truths will only hold you back. Awareness is only the beginning of becoming greater and often is the most difficult. It is amazing that people easily will see a pattern in another person, but be completely blocked to their own behavior. Without being aware, you will not understand the strengths, weaknesses and patterns that you carry with you as you move through life. You will be living in a shadow.

"Your net worth to the world is usually determined by what remains after your bad habits are subtracted from your good ones." —Benjamin Franklin

Developing your self-awareness can be achieved by examining the behavior patterns of how you respond to different situations. If you are brutally honest with yourself, you will be able to track in detail your good and bad reactions. Be your own detective and seek out others for their opinions of your behavior. This is not a sign of weakness, it is a sign of strength. Create your own self-assessment surveys.

WHO ARE YOU AND WHO DO YOU WANT TO BE?

"The only person you are destined to become is the person you decide to be." —Ralph Waldo Emerson

Having a good sense of who you are helps push you into different activity and behavioral goals. By practicing positive awareness, you can excel at what you choose to improve. An understanding of yourself and who you are can help capitalize on your strengths and overcome your weaknesses.

I was an introvert until I practiced the art of communication and now have become an extrovert. I went from uncomfortableness to excitement, by identifying who I was and who I wanted to become. I focused on what practices I could take to get me out of my shell.

Awareness is knowing and accepting your complete person. Your desire to make improvements are yours to grasp and practice permanently.

But you will accomplish nothing unless you take command and thrust forward into awareness.

"Life is not about finding yourself. Life is about creating yourself." —Lolly Daskal

Self-awareness means knowing your values, personality, needs, habits, emotions, strengths and weaknesses. Self-awareness will result in a reduction of stress and fear as you accept who you currently are. This will allow you to create a vision of the person you want to become, both professionally and personally.

Emotional self-awareness is understanding how you react and how your feelings impact your actions or inactions. When you defend all of your actions, you miss out at being aware of what you can learn. You can't defend all your actions. Take responsibility for the negative way you respond to conflicts and differences.

Be aware that someone's differences are just that, differences, and the same holds true for yours.

Your ability to collect evidence from objective reasoning is crucial versus emotional subjective assumptions.

Once you start to perfect this, you will be able to take on more situations that are ambiguous and subjective. At that point your gut feeling will be your problem solver and confidence will prevail in actions. Practice "conflict awareness," and the ability to be detached from an emotional interpretation. This practice will allow you to analyze situations accurately.

AWARENESS IN ACTION

Awareness works if you step outside of yourself and pay attention to your habits and behaviors. Ask others about their perceptions of your behaviors and actions.

"One good mentor can be more informative than a college education and more valuable than a decade's income." —Sean Stephenson

Find a mentor. Growth and change takes humility and courage and most people refuse, or do not know how, to look deep into the foundation of what drives them or brings them down in life. A mentor can help. If you have solid relationships with people that you trust, they will be direct with you and give you an accurate opinion of your behavior; use them. Ask them if you come across as weak, strong, victimized, open-minded, angry, lazy, miserable or set in your ways.

What you don't want to hear might be what you need to hear.

Also, know that if you tell a person that you would like them to be your mentor, you are creating a responsibility in that person. Most people will not take this lightly. By gaining a mentor, you will have an additional—and strong resource to add to your friend arsenal.

When you ask someone to comment on what they perceive to be your good or poor habits or behaviors it is important to not react negatively. This will create a trust that will enable them to continue providing you with useful feedback in the future. The key is to show that you are interested and that you also are open to feedback. This will speed up your ability to identify previously unrecognized poor behaviors and to begin practicing good behaviors.

Keep in mind, your job is to evaluate the incoming information. Examine what is said and start keeping a log.

Compare your views of yourself versus what others think.

You are not providing a platform for someone to tell you how to run your life. Your responsibility is to take control of what you hear, analyze it, accept or reject it, and practice the actions of better behavior.

It is important to have fun with the process of practicing. If you don't, then your weakness will prevail over the practice. Breaking through tough times will be much easier as you grow and build a stronger foundation.

Self-awareness is opening yourself up to what you are aware of, and what you are not. Acceptance of what you control and what you don't will be the hardest concept to embrace. But once this happens, you will live in the solution and not the problem. You don't have all the answers and mistakes will happen.

How you talk, listen and react will be strengthened by your awareness.

Your ability to control yourself will be monumental to your peace and happiness.

"When you're interested in doing something, you do it only when it's convenient. When you're committed to something, you accept no excuses; only results."

—Kenneth Blanchard

AWARENESS QUESTIONS

- Do you have the same consistent outcomes that derail you?
- What regrets do you carry?
- What areas do you want to permanently improve?
- What are your greatest weaknesses?
- What do others see as your biggest weaknesses?
- When do your weaknesses affect you negatively?
- What have you done to conquer your weaknesses?
- Do you compare your views with facts?

- Have you observed someone's poor behav or and said to yourself, "How can they not see that!" Now ask yourself the same question.
- Do you set personal behavioral goals for yourself?

"The unexamined life is not worth living."

—Socrates

Those are powerful and direct words from one of the world's greatest philosophers. No beating around the bush here. Either examine your life, or accept that you live in your eggshell and you are not worth the space you take up. What does that mean to us?

We must become aware of our patterns of behavior or we never will achieve success and what we want out of life.

That is scary. Imagine going through life not understanding why we are acting like we do? Well, 90 percent of us do. That is gut-wrenching, and we are going to end it here with this book.

We must ask ourselves questions, beat ourselves up, interrogate and define our thoughts, actions and words—all to become aware of our patterns of behavior and the actual results they create. We might think our behavior and thoughts are effective and give us the best chance for success, but until we become aware of what our thoughts, behavior and words actually create around us and in others, we are lost in potential.

Take responsibility for your poor actions or inactions.

To justify your bad habits is nothing more than putting Miracle-Gro® on your undesired weeds.

BLAMING

- Blaming someone for the way you are feeling
- Blaming someone for your lack of success
- Blaming the economy for lack of achievement
- Blaming your inability to succeed due to your past
- Blaming your inability to accomplish because of time factors

- Blaming your lack of education
- Blaming your sex or ethnicity
- Blaming a lack of control
- Blaming unfairness
- Blaming a lack of opportunities
- Blaming not being smart enough

Blaming is one of those excuses that we can use for a lifetime. The fact of the matter is we are in control of our own movement, either backward, idle or forward in life. Blaming to avoid moving forward is something that is controllable if we so choose. Excuses and blaming are two parallel words. Identify when you are about to blame someone or something and replace it with a positive action. Be accountable to yourself. Don't give up your power through excuses. Your life is in your hands, not in the box of excuses.

Take time each week to examine your behavior and your words. Most importantly, think of the outcome created. Do you achieve the outcome you want, or do you achieve no outcome, or do you achieve an outcome for the benefit of someone else? Embrace your past as evidence, good or bad.

I am always amazed when people keep repeating the same behavior, and that they are surprised the results are the same.

In order to grow you must be open to the negative and positive spins you give to each and every situation. And you must be aware of these spins. You must become aware of what you can control and what you can't.

Awareness also allows you to let go of a huge albatross: being afraid of being yourself for fear of judgment and criticism.

Fear of being judged is the number one cause of immobility.

Why are you wrong and they are right? How crippling we make our days by not living the way we want and instead living for someone else's ideals and not our own. You have value, you control your world. And once you have opened your mind to this reality, you are on your way to a healthy new mental lifestyle.

#2

"Everything I have been successful with started with uncomfortableness, fearfulness, and fearlessness. Success starts with exactly that: discomfort and second-guessing." —Tim Marshall

I have taught, trained, led and driven people to their greatest pinnacles of permanent success and growth.

I am the guy who has bussed tables and run companies. I set goals and accomplishments that very few people have achieved consistently. I am not talking about coming up with Facebook or Home Depot.

I am talking about an average guy who has overcome obstacles, and during the economic crash of 2008, built one of the fastest growing companies based on percentage growth in America with just a telephone and a desk. I am talking about someone who had such low self-esteem that I muttered words when speaking, but went on to become the number one account sales rep in a globally-recognized company for 14 years straight. And it all started by being myself, doing what was uncomfortable, and relentlessly practicing having a very open mind. ***This works.*** There is no poster child for success, and it is never too early or late to start. It could be being the best house mom to running companies. What do you want to achieve?

What you read above is where you will be when you take the action steps and don't give up. Life is a journey that can end very quickly; take your moments and never forget that you will not have them back. Take control of your freedom and unlock your potential.

I dare you to live your dreams and discover your hidden talents.

You might just become the person you were meant to be, rather than an unfinished puzzle.

THE ULTIMATE

Start becoming aware of opportunities and challenges. Then you can start to envision your path effortlessly.

- The secret is when you think about something enough you ***might*** take action steps to ***actually*** move forward.

However, when you mix your thoughts with positive actions, you will move forward no matter what.

- Becoming aware will open your mind. This will allow you to create new and improved guidelines toward reaching your vision. When you envision and start acting, you will begin to become more aware of your strengths and weaknesses. This will bring excitement, frustration, and potentially overwhelm you. There will be setbacks and victories. Recognizing small victories is key. If you get ahead of yourself and start thinking too far into the future, you won't accomplish what you need to accomplish today. They all are building blocks toward your vision. So be sensitive to yourself and the ebb and flow of small victories; be patient and practice your vision.

#3

BREAKING FEAR WITH AN OPEN MIND

DON'T KEEP WONDERING WHAT YOU COULD HAVE

"When you start to practice awareness and begin envisioning your goals, you will begin to break through your fear." —Tim Marshall

Practicing an open mind is a core principle that you must ingest, understand and act on. Without an open mind, we project either negative or positive outcomes, often to our detriment.

Until you understand that you give your surroundings both negative and positive projections, it will be difficult to open your mind. Your mind must be open to differentiate the two! Your projections are controlled by your mind. We pretend to be in situations, we pretend our own reality. To grow and have balance you must be open to the negative and positive spins you give to every situation; and you must be aware of these spins. Limit the distractions around you and these distraction, or "Zingers" will be kept at bay! Zingers knock you off track, off balance, out of focus. They are mental detours from the truth—they may send you down the wrong path or just cause you to react poorly.

Both positive and negative projections can be controlled by your awareness, and how you identify your situations and the people around you.

Balance and growth cannot happen without recognizing and then detaching outside distractions.

Limiting these distractions and giving them less weight in your life will change your core way of life. Act on the distractions fast and precisely and keep them away from you.

People usually cause distractions, but that is not true for everything. Other distractions can be an act of god such as the weather or media with events that come and go that draw us in and can create distractions.

THE HURRICANE

Living in Florida, I was put in several situations that would cause me to either lose focus or detach and move forward even harder. A hurricane was headed our way. I saw the reactions of many around me as the drama unfolded. Most of the work activity came to a screeching holt. I was aware of the hurricane and did take precautions "as I should," but I knew I had no control over the outcome. I was not going to control the hurricane.

It hit us, and the damage was extensive but not catastrophic. In my area, the power cables were completely taken and there was no air conditioning. My house was a humid 95 degrees, everything was a watery mess, and the office was all but empty. But I did not allow myself to lose my focus. At the time, I was an account manager/sales rep. I knew most competitors were either complacent or mentally effected by the major "zinger," the hurricane, and that many businesses were either closed or running on generators.

I will start with the first word that came to mind: Relentless. I walked into the office and noticed that there was only a skeleton staff of employees who wanted to work. As I sat down at my desk, I wrote down one sentence: The only limitations I have are in my mind. And then I went on a tear. I went to as many potential customers as possible in each day. Some were closed, but the ones that were open gave me the opportunity to spend time with the key decision makers. They were battling on...and I could help them. We problem-solved, and I was able to justify changing some of their office technology so that after the storm cleanup they would be at peak performance. At the time, the average quota in my business was $40,000. I sold $425,000 that month and accounted for 95 percent of the total sales for the company. My success proves that when you apply detaching yourself from distractions, not projecting negativity and staying relentlessly focused, you can achieve anything.

When you practice having an open mind, you will learn one huge game changer: We cannot change anyone or any situation we have no control over, period. We can only let others know how their behavior affects us and then it is up to them to either want to make the changes or not.

If we try to change others and they keep acting the same, resentment and anger follows, and this thwarts our path to an open mind.

You can't waste your valuable time trying to control how others behave and live their lives! Your time is invaluable. Once it passes you will never get it back. Concentrate on yourself and how your actions lead to positive fulfillment. Don't worry about the other guy, and you will start to change and identify new ideas and actions that clear your mind from contaminated thoughts and allow you to truly live your life.

THE TITANIC OF EMOTIONS

Our emotions can take us down a path of uncontrolled anger and irrational thinking, the exact opposite of what we are trying to achieve.

We bank too much on our feelings, at the expense of our possible outcomes. Quantify the ways you react to negative situations. Is fear causing you to lose your focus? Your emotions can gloss over vulnerabilities and protect you from reality; for example, saying one thing but feeling another way. One of the best ways to review your emotional reactions is to track it with evidence.

Write down how you handled a situation, or if you can, tape-record your description of the event. Wait a day. Then review what you wrote. Is that how you want to act? Think about what your reactions were, versus the way you would handle it now when you have control of your emotions and you are not shutting down your mind with resistance and walls. This will take practice. But you will notice that the meanings we put on things are either grossly overstated/overreacted and/or due to a communication coming our way that we attached to ourselves with a closed mind — rather than accepting with an open mind, and then analyzing why this communication was occurring.

Answer these questions to help you understand why an open mind is so important.

- Are your emotions consistently getting in the way of your focus? If so, you are giving too much meaning to the situation and you are the only one responsible for that attention.

- Is your behavior a positive action and/or is your behavior a punishing action? Ask yourself what is the purpose of your reaction and how will it benefit you. If it cannot benefit you and it is punishing, then you have just closed your mind entirely and are guilty of being the problem, whether you are in the right or wrong. It is all perspective — and you must have an open mind to see perspective.

- Do you feel you have control over the situation or the person? Be careful with this, because here is where we go down the rabbit hole. Just like Alice in Wonderland you cannot control someone's emotions, only your own. If you can't control, then let go and detach; it takes practice and must be practiced often. It works only if you are aware.

- Once you lose control of your emotions, you lose no matter what. Firmness is a gift that one acquires through the practice of controlling one's emotions. Firmness and directness prevail always.

I had a good employee who constantly got caught up in his emotions. He would send emotional emails, overanalyzing most situations. The emails were almost daily and were very depressing to others. I requested that he take the time to backtrack three weeks and read all the emails that he had sent out and then discuss them with me. This exercise caused him to gain awareness. Until then he had not realized that his emotions were constantly undermining his intentions, and he stopped this negative behavior.

YOUR MOST IMPORTANT RELATIONSHIP IS WITH YOURSELF

As you read through the pages of this book, I will reveal some very good strategies to increase your odds of effective communications and actions, which will lead to an open mind and overcoming your fears.

This book is not about exercise or eating healthy but rather feeding your mind so that you can problem-solve better through the art of communication and action.

Taking care of your body will help you as I can attest. As you read this, I am constantly battling the foods I eat and the time I devote to exercise. I am amid a slow breakthrough due to my practice of healthy actions. Physically I am becoming my actions — and I feel great.

FULL THROTTLE

You walk across a bridge to get to the other side. But if you stand at one side of the bridge and stare across and analyze and second-guess yourself — for example, the safety of the situation, why you need to cross that bridge, maybe you could do it tomorrow — then you might not cross.

My point is that in life we have to calculate. What is on the other side of the bridge? Is there something there that you would like to achieve or discover? This is not about just making blind leaps; it is about being decisive in building a foundation for yourself with practiced behavior that will create a balanced and strong foundation in your relationship with yourself. To say that this is not relevant would be to say that a robot can conduct your life better without all the wonderful emotions that we experience in life.

The more strength you have in your decisiveness the more equipped you will be in your relationships, wealth, and career.

With this you will create your own decisive agenda. You will break your fears with decisive action. Cross that bridge.

SOME HELPFUL HINTS

- You have a purpose (an agenda) and so does everyone else. Understanding yourself, and being decisive, will allow you to detach from taking on someone else's agenda, bad mood or lack of consideration. For example, if you are focusing on a project and another person does not, accept it and do not allow that behavior to influence your direction. If you do, then you are now dependent on someone to make you fulfilled or happy.

- People's actions toward you are not necessarily about you, but about them. It isn't about you unless there is clear evidence that you did something that was detrimental or inconsiderate to them. If there is no evidence of this, then it is not your problem.

- Your detachment from someone's actions is achieved by understanding that you cannot control their behavior toward you, you can only ask them to treat you the way you would like. I can try to change someone and try and try again. How am I going to accomplish that if they do not want to change? Then this grows into fearing the behavior before it even starts. If the behavior is extremely damaging to you, then let them know. If they decide to change then great, and if they don't, then the ball is in your court to accept them for who they are or remove yourself from the situation.

- Understanding the above will give you more mental energy and your coping skills will be reinforced by sound judgment, and openness, to start your days.

UNLEASH YOUR WILL—STARTING YOUR MORNING

- Take this moment and cherish it
- Grip the happiest thought you can think of
- Take a breath and exhale slowly
- This is the moment to replace doubt with excitement
- This is the moment that the unthinkable becomes thinkable
- This is the moment you reach your hand out to help another
- This is the day you will be the happiest no matter what hits you

- This is the day you will achieve anything you put your mind to
- This is the day you will never forget it!

The overwhelming challenge for a person is the constant struggle with themselves, but most of us do not take the time to recognize this struggle or influence it for the positive. To initiate this, let's address the most important time of the day: when you wake in the morning.

Each morning is the birth of a new opportunity to practice positive actions through the rest of the day.

I personally divide my day into three parts: 6 a.m. to 12 p.m., 12 to 6 p.m., and 6 p.m. on. This gives three different windows in which to win small victories. And if a window is a setback, you have two other windows to be positive, rather than one event ruining your day.

Starting your morning with a clear head is vital. It is unrealistic to think we can just wake up with a clear mind every morning, although it is possible and ideal. But most of us are carrying a garbage bag of thoughts, usually negative.

Decide if your garbage bag of thoughts is already overflowing, blocking you from being open to your potential for that day. If so, then before you even start your day, your ability to take on anything new or be open to new ideas and actions will already be limited. Try to dump some of that garbage the night before. Make a simple list every night:

- List 2 new good things about your day
- List 2 self-defeating fears about your day
- List 1 wish:"I wish I had this in my life."
- List 2 things you are grateful for in your day
- List 2 positive actions you will practice tomorrow

When you wake the next morning, look at this list calmly and analytically. Discard the frustrations — that was yesterday, don't let it interfere with today. Look at the two truths. Are these truths ugly truths or good truths? If they are bad ones, then look at the behavior that caused them. Don't repeat that behavior today. Look at your two proposed actions — will they help you accomplish your two hopes and dreams? Hopefully this answer will be yes. If it is not, then change them. Lastly, look at the two items that you were thankful for having experienced. Hold those for a few moments, like a shiny trophy of the feelings you can achieve today!

When you write two new good things about your day, remember that we are only as good as how we act. Have fun with the gift of newness, and remember you are unique ; no one on the planet is like you. That's why it is so important to remember the good, and foster the new. You can achieve almost anything that you put your mind to at any given moment.

Embrace the new and practice the good.

Let me go a little further with this.

By writing down the two self-defeating fears about ***your*** day, you become aware of them and now you are in charge of replacing the self-defeating fears with positive actions. The smallest victory could be life-changing.

"I wish I had this in my life": Why not you? How bad do you want it? Sprinkle seeds of wish and start planting them. To allow growth, you must practice watering them, and when you see the first signs of life reaching out of the soil remember that this is your beginning and your miracle that you can grow into one of the most beautiful trees in the world. Never pass on what you can create for yourself. If you do, then the seeds will be carried around for the rest of your life never having the ability to grow.

Two things you're grateful for in your day: What is it that you have in your life that you are grateful for. Life is fantastic if we see the good in what we have.

Two positive actions that you will practice tomorrow: What good is our ability if we don't use it and practice the independence of being an individual? Bettering your situation is one of the greatest and most fulfilling experiences you can have in your life.

THE 30-MINUTE SECRET TO BEING ASTUTE AND SAVVY

You will be amazed at how knowledgeable you will become in a very short time. I have known readers who knew as much after just 30 days as people who had been in an industry for years. And education makes you more open to new knowledge.

- **Increase your knowledge.** But you must practice what you learn. Otherwise, there will be no benefit.

- **Decrease your "phantom thoughts," or anxiousness.** The more information you learn the more engaged and confident you will be. Second-guessing yourself will become less and less as you learn more. It is almost like having a big brother or big sister to back you up!

- **Recognize opportunities**. You will begin to acknowledge strengths and weaknesses.

- **Increase your income.** Learn more and your value goes up. Learn more and your confidence goes up. Learn more and live by what you learn and your income goes up!

#4

IF YOU PRACTICE, CHANGE WILL COME

Let me start by saying, I don't believe in selling change. Practice causes change.

Practice is a lifelong effort; once you stop you will stop growing. There is no graduation from this process, but consistent positive actions lead to great moments. There are only stepping stones to a better understanding of yourself. Patience backed by practice leads to positive actions that will build an indestructible foundation.

The goal is to build a solid foundation of fulfillment and achievement on your terms. A fulfilling life is doing what you want to do; by practicing your given right to grow your greatest asset...***you***! Remember, you will stay consistent with what you practice if you are doing what you want to do. That is why it is so important to practice an open mind. When you dream at night, you "dream," but when you live out your own practiced performance, it will be your greatest reality.

Your life reflects your actions and inactions. No action is an action. Based on how much you practice learning from people, resources, and challenges, this can make you incredibly strong if you keep trying, or incredibly weak if you surrender. The more you practice learning, the more diverse and educated you will be.

My first job out of college was in sales. I had to learn how to prospect and cope with rejection. I relentlessly read books, articles, and listened to CDs and remained on a steady course, ***never turning back to my comfort zone.*** In this new challenge, I began to fail and fail again. I made thousands of phone calls and cold calls, business to business. It was brutal, horrible, uncomfortable, embarrassing and humiliating. But it made me the most powerful salesperson in the company; then before I had a chance to understand my success, I became the top rep in the country year after year. The brutal days became amazing achievements. I also became so intuitive to critical thinking that my creativity took off, and so did my will to teach others what I had learned.

Be active, and act out what you have researched, paralleled with putting relentless effort into the task at hand.

So-called setbacks are wonderful because that's when you start to learn the most.

The more setbacks the better you will become at handling your challenge. I acted out, making 100s of calls a day until I became so comfortable and educated that my results were unprecedented.

It takes 18 months to truly make permanent strides that can lead you to permanent behavior. Be your own coach, counselor, motivator, and most importantly, ***be your own educator.***

Simply reading can give huge benefits. Some people have spent a lifetime of learning and doing their own research on specific subjects. ***Take the opportunity to learn from them.*** Read in the morning. This starts your day with an open mind and new information. Reading exercises your mind to open new ideas to start your day. If you play golf or if you play any sports, or if you are going to take a test, you would practice before leaping into the event, right? Reading in the morning is that practice, and it can boost you into a lifetime of awareness.

THE ULTIMATE IN VERSATILITY—PRACTICE

Thomas Edison failed 1,000 times before creating the light bulb. It was not failure, it was practice.

Practice is not just for a given time. It is for a lifetime. There is no graduation, only stepping stones to better understand your potential.

KEYS TO PRACTICE

- **A concentrated effort to improve** - Practice takes awareness, open-mindedness and kindness on your part. I practice daily embracing those around me and try to give myself to them without expecting returns. That is one of my practices that I live by and will never change. Make a practice list that motivates you to lead your greatest asset, you.

- **An understanding that there is no Graduation** - As stated above, I often see these bursts of improvements from people only for them to go back right where they started. They stop practicing their new actions, then the open mind door closes and so does their platform of practicing. Next comes the complaining and the deflation of being stuck in a life they don't want. So here it is again: ***Practice and practice.*** You will not find it overwhelming, you will find it satisfying as you see the positive results.

- **A decision means nothing unless you put your decision into action** - Some people preach that all you need to do is decide. OK, I get that, and that is important if you have a concrete decision such as driving to the store or quitting a job. But most decisions are only initiations of new actions that must be practiced with action for decisions to take shape. So remember, a decision is only as good as the effort you put into transforming it into a reality.

- **Mistakes are a part of practicing** - Einstein did not come up with his theory of relativity overnight Who really knows how many attempts it took to get the exact calculation, but when he did, it changed his world and ours. So, embrace challenges and learn from them, build on them, they will give you great character if you never give up.

- **Avoid resolution dates** - Practice your decision now, and continue practicing every day. Be careful on due dates, they are good and necessary but we are humans, and humans make future promises often, without following through with action. And then when the date comes and goes, we discard the goal. New Year's resolutions are only good if you practice the resolution. But if you are looking for a way to give up on the resolution, a due date provides you with the perfect vehicle.

- **Have fun practicing; your competition is you!** This is such a great way to strive for amazing results in your life. Don't worry about the other guy, worry about your own goals and desires. If you hit a golf ball poorly, it affects your score card, not the other person's. And when you do well, you beat the you from yesterday! And you are a winner today.

Practice allows you to make your life more organized and achievable. You need more than just your own experiences to achieve success, so you must be relentless in learning and experience new adventures. This is a form or practice.

How can you be successful at something that you don't understand fully?

To understand, you must prepare, and that preparation includes research from every available outside source. Books, people, the Internet, interest groups, chat rooms, social media are all fantastic learning centers.

When you are prepared, your ***fear*** and ***stress*** comes down and the mind becomes lighter, open, and confident. You become less emotional.

You become more open to fresh ideas, rather than being fearful. Other people are a great resource. Their experiences could be drastically different from yours, so why not learn insights from another person. Positive or negative, they are equally beneficial to you.

Quality people will be more open to vulnerability, and closed-minded people are stuck in their own protected thoughts.

When you practice being less fearful of your vulnerabilities you will be able to focus on positives and not the negatives.

The drain of building the barriers around you will end. If you get uncomfortable, recognize that as growth and continue the practice of always moving forward.

This will create momentum. Momentum can be a beautiful open wave that lasts a lifetime. You create your own momentum, no one else does. You can be inspired by someone, but it is hollow unless you act upon that inspiration. Be your own momentum counselor.

Momentum is not that hard to keep going once you have the open mind and mental energy to back up inspirations with action.

There are no such things as slumps unless you become content, passive, overconfident, and close-minded. I build my momentum by fearlessly going after a project or goal. One action breeds more action. Discomfort tells me I am challenging myself and that gives me extraordinary reinforcement. I will not stop until I know I have completed the task at hand to the best of my ability, or I have added to my lifestyle.

#5

MR. MIND, TEAR DOWN THIS WALL

MAKE YOUR LIFE RICHER THAN EVER BEFORE

What is a wall? It's a verb and it's a noun. In its common verb form, it means to enclose a space — maybe to protect and maybe to afford privacy — to wall yourself in. Is it useful? Absolutely! The problem? Sometimes we get caught up in the noun form of wall. That definition is a vertical meant to divide, typically from fear.

Understand the difference? If not, then think of this: "walled in' can contain strength and a sense of self; a "wall" usually divides us from some other entity. For our purposes, let's further define the two. You can be walled in a fortress of strength and the realization of your own worth, fortified against others' judgments. And you lead your life from this center of power. Or we can erect walls that divide us from seeing the other side. They divide us from feeling what's on the other side, they divide us from embracing people and experiences.

Finally, walls divide us from opportunities that are right in front of us, but on the other side of "the wall." The walls are there, inside us, and most often exist in the noun form. Then we build several of these walls and we end up "walled in," in a prejudicial manner, closed from outside thoughts.

We also can be prisoners. Prisoners of our negative thinking, prisoners of too much bad thinking, prisoners of what we haven't accomplished. Our walls are thick. Before you go on, stop and make sure you understand the difference. Ours are not happy, useful walls. Our walls prevent us from reaching through to make positive changes as resistance can. How does resistance keep us from passing through the wall? Resistance is the reverse of moving forward. Its creator? Negative perception, ascribed meaning without evidence, projection of fears, and lack of objective thinking. Your resistance may be all of those, or just a few. It's time to recognize them.

What's the purpose you might ask? The purpose of going through the negative barriers/resistance is to open your mind.

Open your mind to see positive resources inside yourself.

Open your mind to build a foundation of new experiences and better relationships. We do this through ***practice***. Will there by an "AH-HA" moment? Maybe, maybe not. Practice means being ***aware*** of your resistance. The awareness will break down the wall. Your experiences are stepping stones. They are learning experiences. Use them.

Did you act on good actions and practice . . . integrity, preparation, being kind, working hard and staying focused? Did you give it everything you could? Or did you move forward with bad actions and no practice. Did you "wing it," blame others, and not accept accountability.

We can review what we accomplished and how the outcome was effected based on good or bad actions and learn from these behaviors. Your awareness of resistance will move you forward. Forward to new ideas, exciting challenges, opportunities. You will become attuned to your resistance radar, and recognize the resulting poor behaviors and actions in the past. Life is a sell...so you might as well be successful.

Ask yourself if you feel walled in. Take a job/career. Most people feel dependent, controlled by the need to be employed, which is very important, but we can get imprisoned by what we have to do versus what we want to do. And we let that build into a wall. But it doesn't have to be this way. Start making a list of the action steps that you can do to change your career or job into something that you desire versus something that you feel forced to do each day. If you ***learn*** more by researching, if you ***give*** more than what is asked, and if you ***organize*** yourself better, your new actions will turn into small victories. This will put you in control. If you're not recognized, and your practices are not met with opportunities, be patient. If you expect and/or try to get your company to give you more; then the reverse will happen, and you will be stuck behind the wall.

One example of a very poor behavior that occurs from building up a wall is when you feel you are not given what you deserve in business. I have seen this so many times... When an employee does not get their way, they will intentionally hold back and not perform up to their ability in a form of protest. The only thing that is accomplished here is that you are holding yourself back and hurting your opportunities to grow. I have seen many salespeople turn off their activity button to rebel against the company, which means they will sell less or purposely not work hard enough to sell at all. They think they are making a point but, meanwhile, they are losing money and creating a bigger hole for themselves. They are self-sabotaging their days. Humans are not perfect, nor are companies.

If you feel you are living under a radical injustice, then find a better company to work for, but never lose your will to achieve.

The same holds true with relationships. If you are always looking for someone to make you happy, then you are walling yourself in and dependent on someone else. The key to a great relationship is to have low expectations, because that is where the freedom comes in and the fear of disappointment becomes a non-issue.

#6

UNIQUELY MINE: ABOUT MY WALL

"TIM MARSHALL"

I was 19 and working in a dead-end job. College was for other people —people who were smart — people better and different from me. I spent my days working and nights partying. One day I woke up to the upsetting realization that all my party buddies had deserted me. I was discouraged and felt defeated. "What happened to me and the time that had past? Where did my so-called friends go?" I didn't want to accept it, but they were growing and I was not. After judging and railing against the injustice of it all, I was presented with a choice: keep closing myself in and feel sorry for myself, which was nothing new, or try to open my mind and understand the situation for what it truly was. I chose to open my mind. That single good decision, although mired in the muck of my old negative thinking, turned my life around. (Although it did start with the bad news that my entrance test at a local community college scored my aptitude at a seventh-grade level. More on what actions I took later.)

UNIQUELY YOURS: ABOUT YOUR WALL, [YOUR NAME]

Look at your surroundings. Are you a victim of what surrounds you? Are you dissatisfied? Do you feel you have no control? Do you feel that if only your surroundings will change, your life will get better? Well, guess what.

No matter how much you change the geography, you still bring *you* with you.

Analyze your behavior. Try to step truly outside yourself and observe how you come across to others. How do you interact in situations? How do you perceive people, situations and most importantly yourself? Are you reacting to situations based on your past experiences and projected outcomes, rather than understanding and ***accepting*** the current situation?

It all starts with awareness. You have to accept the good and bad as it comes along, but you don't have to sink your teeth into the bad.

As you start looking at small changes you want to make in yourself, *awareness* is the key word.

Be aware of the good, the bad, and the projected bad. Everything starts with being aware of patterns, thoughts, actions, immobility, fear, overwhelming thoughts and those catastrophic projections.

A BUILDUP OF BARNACLES

If you run from pain or from a bad experience and bury it deep, you just created a barnacle, and as the years pass, so does the buildup of your barnacles. Barnacles attach themselves to a hard surface and then cement themselves, oozing more and more cement over time, until they are firmly attached. Through reproduction, they create more barnacles.

Some of us are covered in barnacles and don't realize it. Someone could be aware of the barnacles but doesn't know how to remove them. It starts with one barnacle. I can have barnacles that I am not aware of, or I can be aware of my barnacles, but view them as permanent. In either case, you are like a boat, slowed down by the barnacles on your hull, and wasting energy trying to move forward despite the drag of the barnacles.

But here is the great news: You can rid yourself of barnacles by finding the place where they are attached. But first you must be aware of the barnacles.

#7

PRIMITIVE POWER

CONTROLLING OUR WORDS

Let's start with something simple. What comes out of your mouth? Is it judgmental? Is it toxic? Is it kind? Would someone else describe your words as verbally negative or more positive? What comes out of your mouth is a direct reflection of what's going on in your brain. If you want to control something, our words are the only thing in our life that we have complete control over; so, let's start there.

How do we control our words better? By being aware of our patterns and why we say the things we say. Our words are a result of our thoughts. What are our thoughts a result of? They are a result of our current inactions, actions, ***and*** our experiences. This combination leads us to harboring a projected outcome —even before we process the moment. That's paralysis — our minds are closed to the different possibilities of what could happen rather than on what has happened, and that defines the moment. It is simply impossible to be open-minded when we have already projected the outcome.

Then there is the fear factor.

Most of us are afraid of being ourselves for fear of judgment and of criticism, perceived or real, from others. We envy those who appear not to have this trait, but we don't ask ourselves why they can be carefree and I can't. So, change your oral behavior — it is totally within your control and you can practice it simply and easily. Being mindful of your words is the most important awareness you can have.

Practice speaking your mind with positive intentions.

Everything that we do in life is practice. Look at new people and situations as a fresh positive turning point in your life. How do you do this? Read out loud and practice your clear pronunciation. Stand in front of a mirror and practice. Yes, that is right. Talk to the mirror like it is a person. Ask upbeat questions. Create fearlessness.

Even if you have to pretend at first, soon you will find that just practicing talking in an upbeat positive fashion will change the way you communicate in real life.

Practice for three five-minute periods during the day.

After three days, try your routine in real life. You are not judging the person you are talking to, and you are holding back your projected outcomes. You are trying to ike the person by projecting positive words toward that person. If you have a friend you like, pretend you are talking to that person.

You will be surprised at the results. Communications become friendlier, and strangely, in most cases, you will find yourself liking that person. In turn, this will push you into situations that you would normally shy away from. If you feel awkward or uncomfortable, that is a sign that you need to practice being in that situation more if it is positive. Perhaps start your new method of communicating with someone you feel you will like. Try that a few times and see what happens.

The most remarkable success you can achieve is controlling the words that come out of your mouth and, in today's world, the texts you send.

A negative text stings more than words, because it continually sits there in black and white, rather than receding into foggy memory. Once you have begun to control your words, move on to texts, which are easier to change.

With a vigilant effort, especially when you are reactive and upset, control your texts. Do not react negatively.

Keep your personal words to your own private circle.

Have a small group of confidants you can trust. When you release too much information to those who are not in your defined circle, then you are open for misinterpretation, judgment, and sabotage. Be you, but be smart and genuine. Make your life easier by practicing the discipline of holding your words for those who can care for them.

At that point, you will have achieved one remarkable success already, and a major breakthrough that you may or may not realize: now your actions, in this case your words, are diminishing the power of your past experiences, diminishing your old projected outcome. Remember what controlled your thoughts — your past experiences and current actions. Now, at least with your words, your current actions soon will become your past experiences. Your new actions, now wedded to your recent past positive experiences, begin to dictate positive thoughts. Now you will have started the chain reaction toward the development of a truly open mind.

LUCID ANALYSIS

Six People Can Interpret One Topic Six Different Ways.

An open mind will allow you to understand this. You project your understanding onto someone. But that is not their reality. Their reality is based on their experiences — not yours. The result: Your words can be completely misinterpreted. Sometimes the best way to get your point across is to use an analogy that the person you are speaking to would understand. In other words, enter their reality, rather than force your reality on them. Emotions are tied to a day's events. Sometimes communication is best matched with parallel emotions, so pick and choose your time for maximum emotional compatibility.

A SIMPLE WORDS TO-DO LIST

Practice is the key to being a great communicator.

1. Practice speaking less about yourself. When you listen more you learn more and you see more. Everyone you meet is a resource to learn from, but if you do all of the talking, then you are living only between your two ears. Conversations should be split equally if possible.

2. Practice being your humble self. The surest way to be understood by others is to be the real you. If you act differently, then you will get a response directed at a mask you created, and this will denigrate the lines of communication and not foster a real relationship.

3. Practice reducing vulgarity and slang.. The cleaner your language, the less you will offend. Studies have shown that the less swear words and the more specific vocabulary, the more you are respected. Even if someone uses vulgarity and profanity, you should not follow suit.

4. Practice not interrupting. Practice not being a sentence jumper. Do you like being interrupted in the middle of a sentence? The same holds true for the other person. These interruptions occur when you only listen to a fraction of a conversation and then go into "think mode" to figure out the fastest way to respond without even processing the entire message. Number one, it is rude, and number two, it leads to poor comprehension. A battle to be understood ensues.

5. Practice not gossiping. This can only lead to bad feelings all the way around. Treat people the way you would like to be treated.

6. Practice not being negative. Bring up positive news and thoughts. Don't reinforce the bad or intimate the negative because you could create a black cloud around you that will push people away.

7. Practice being brief. Be specific and condense your points. Your message will be clear and the recipient will be better engaged. If you create a trail that goes in different directions and circles around, then the person might get lost in the woods.

8. Practice being polite if the person is negative or rude. It's not about you. It is their projection. Do not join it. Detach yourself and don't engage. You will only do yourself a disservice.

9. Practice communicating without judgment. Prejudgments are just your own projections. Be open-minded. Do not force your judgments on to another. Don't try to convince someone about their own feelings. Listen.

The above list applies to CEOs or panhandlers. It is important to practice communication manners at all times.

The better you conduct yourself, the less *fear* you will have second-guessing your behavior.

FASTEN YOUR SEATBELT

Now practice communicating with people who make you feel uncomfortable.

This is another step in your forward movement. Remember — you can control your words better than anything else in your life. So, perfect it.

Go right back to the mirror for a five-minute session beforehand and pretend you are talking to that person. As you keep practicing, you will achieve a growing comfort level, and you will start to open up and listen more as opposed to protecting your feelings and allowing that person to have control over you.

FEAR OF PUBLIC SPEAKING

The second-most common fear is speaking in front of others. (The number one fear is flying). Actually, some people might call it "the terror" of speaking in front of others. So, let me go on a little tangent here.

You have learned to control your words, now you might end up in a position where you are speaking to a group. But your brain sends out warning shots. Why? Simple — judgement. You are afraid of being judged.

My first prepared speech began with a mutter, my head down, intensely reading every word from a prepared sheet as I hid behind the podium. I might have glanced up once or twice in terror only to see all eyes upon me. The reality is this behavior was rooted in long-held self-esteem issues which had developed into terror of speaking to strangers. I hid from this and avoided it at all cost.

First, I began the practice of controlling my words with friends. Next, I practiced controlling my words with “unfriendlies.” Finally, I took the plunge of speaking to groups. My platform of practice served me well. While I wasn’t comfortable, I was OK. And when I realized that no one was judging me, they were mostly in their own world, I actually relaxed.

From then until now I have practiced consistently to do what is uncomfortable —communicating with people at every opportunity as a means of practice. Now my fear of communicating has turned into excitement. By starting out with practice, and weathering the small storms of doing what I feared, I set the tone of fearless energy in my speech-giving. It took time and practice, but at this point I will get in front of any size audience and deliver a natural genuine image of myself because my practice allowed me to enter my comfort zone.

Start somewhere but keep practicing; you will find yourself at ease and eventually will be eager to speak more and more. One of the best activities to practice is reading out loud. This will exercise your vocal cords and your pronunciation of words that will become clearer. Practice the inflection in your voice to capture the most important points of what you read.

This applies to you. Practice. One person, two people, three people, a group of people. It does not matter.

Just take the plunge.

There will be discomfort, but I promise you that your practice sessions will build and build. You will be practicing what you feel is uncomfortable, but that will pass. Start somewhere, but keep practicing; you eventually will find yourself at ease and eventually will be eager to speak more. One of the best activities to practice is reading out loud. This will exercise your vocal cords and your pronunciation of words. Practice with stretching your words to enhance the inflection in your voice to capture the most important points of what you read.

A FEW SIMPLE QUESTIONS TO HELP YOU IN PUBLIC SPEAKING

- How good are your communication skills?
- Do you feel confident in speaking/talking?
- Are you persuasive and understandable?
- Are you consistent in your message?
- Do you ramble?
- Do you use voice inflection?

The way you communicate with people will create an immediate perception of you. If you sound squeaky, shy, nervous and anything but confident, you will be judged poorly. That is why it is so important to practice speaking, reading, and voice inflection. Judgment occurs the moment you open your mouth to speak, and clarity will be analyzed immediately. Children are a great example of using speaking and voice inflection to get what they want. As adults, we become more conservative in our speaking because for fear of making a mistake or being judged. Research and confidence go together, and when it comes to speaking, the more you know the more comfortable you are when delivering your message. So, you need two traits when publicly speaking: It is imperative to know your subject matter, and practice delivering the message so your voice and presence is commanding. If you sound high-pitched or monotone, you immediately do not sound confident. When you become a persuasive speaker, even the most useless topics sound interesting. In the beginning of this book, I discussed saying your name ...This is your beginning point. Practice it until your name sounds like other names you hear that are in the spotlight. A practice and listening technique is watching TV and listening to the different actors, news anchors or anyone who is in front of large audiences to express their message. Listen and digest the differences from voice to voice, and identify where you fit in and how would you sound if you were on TV.

Power is built through our communications; it is not always what we say but how we say it.

If you want, emulate one of the announcers. I have spent years reading out loud — it is easy and helps your pronunciations and your projections.

Passion and enthusiasm come with practice and your ability to have the will to improve your techniques. Pronunciation is something that must be practiced, along with slowing your speech down so that you do not run your words over someone's ability to comprehend them.

A SIMPLE COMMUNICATION TO-DO LIST

- ***Practice introducing yourself.*** This will lead to people remembering you as opposed to playing a guessing game of trying to remember who you are, what your name is, and getting you confused with someone else. This also signifies you have confidence. The goal is to be recognized by your name.

- ***Practice knowing something about the other person.*** Most of us like to be recognized and have someone know something about us. This brings out good will and shows the person you care. Friendships and business relationships start here.

- ***Practice making eye contact.*** A must! This instills respect and confidence.

- ***Practice smiling.*** You are much more approachable when you smile. You are projecting "welcome" and interest to another person.

BREAK OUT OF YOUR ROUTINE

What do you need to do to further the process of opening your mind?

Just like you did with your words, break out of your routine.

Routines are not good or bad, they are just limiting.

And to achieve an open mind you must embrace fresh experiences. Call it stimuli, call it a jolt, call it whatever you want —just do it.

Experience the wonder of different things! Small things, big things. It doesn't matter. Just do something different. Trying different things creates an excitement within you — you extend and open the profile that is you. Speaking classes, language classes, downloads, the career that you might someday want to switch to — immerse yourself in new possibilities.

Take simple actions steps that will open your mind a bit, and that will let you begin to see the world as other people do. Take a panoramic look at books, people, travel — what can you expose yourself to? What new thing can you introduce into your life? Maybe you try a different genre of music or books. Perhaps you travel someplace you have never been. It could be a local park or Brazil!

Perhaps you take a deep breath and befriend somebody that always annoyed you. It doesn't matter! The point is try something out of the box — out of the box of you! This will create new desires, habits, and start redefining who you are. This will stimulate your senses and increase your awareness.

Look at yourself — thoroughly. Why are you close-minded? Are you prejudiced? What judgments about situations and locations have been predetermined before you were even exposed to them? Push yourself in new ways! Just start somewhere.

If listening to a new type of music seems too reckless, then do something simple like trying a new food. Try a new morning routine where you stretch for 10 minutes. Try a new gas station. Go to the local park or dog park. Look up your new food, the new genre of music, the career that you might someday want to switch to — immerse yourself in new possibilities. These simple actions will open your mind vastly, and let you begin to see the world as other people do, rather than projecting yourself on their world. Staying in the same routine for a long period makes your brain a closed vessel, within which you always feel in control of your surroundings. The old expression, "Go with what you know," is a horrible way to approach life. It allows you to put on blinders, and live isolated from the reality of others.

What makes us so serious after our youth? We get locked into routines and responsibilities, but those are something that we can control. And, in fact, your routine could be adding needless responsibilities to your life. This is the point where people lose themselves and wonder why they are not happy.

The key is detaching from the weight of life by breaking out of our routine.

New opportunities and doors will open as you explore new avenues. And maybe you will have a more objective view of the old routines and which ones are productive and which are not.

The more you give to yourself, the more you will get back.

It is not a bad thing to have routines, in fact it is vital to consistency. But not trying new routines or experiences does not let you see what your life could turn into.

It is important to recognize and examine your routines.

Are they motivating or demotivating? For example: I have never heard someone complain if they become physically fit from training five times a week. But I have heard people complain if they drink or eat too much five times a week.

It is easy to break out of your routine and get involved. Any Internet search will reveal interesting groups right in your area!

- Meditation and Yoga Groups
- Book Club and Poetry Groups
- Art Groups
- Singles Groups
- Couples Groups
- Pottery and Art Groups
- Fitness Boot Camps
- Small Business Groups
- Nature Groups
- Cycling Groups
- Dog or Pet Event Groups

- Adventure and Sport Groups
- Painting Groups
- Music Clubs
- Real Estate Investor Groups
- Photography Groups
- Motorcycle Groups
- Salsa Dancing Groups

#8

DON'T BE A PRISONER OF YOUR OWN PERCEPTIONS

To truly have an open mind, we need to see past physical appearances and practice communicating with others whom we initially might not believe we share any common interests.

Different people, all genders, race, job positions, income classes. Using differences to close your mind off to others is a way to lift yourself up by putting others down. We all want the same things: respect, love, and justice, and to live life on our terms without judgment.

The greatest joy for me is to go any place and make friends with any person by being kind and respecting who they are. It could be a gas station attendant, waitress, CPA, tow truck driver, street sweeper, anyone. We all are unique and all are rich in experiences. Why not be a vampire and suck in others' experiences and see if they apply to your life, your success?

The more people you can relate with, the more information you will gain through osmosis which, in turn, will help you grow personally, financially, educationally, and corporately. You learn from books —well why can't you learn from the experiences of the millions of people around you, whether they are rich or poor, esteemed by society or not.

There was a workman fixing my electric gate. His uniform had the dank look of a man who had spent 10 hours out in the Florida sun. And his hands were caked in oil and dirt, his face needed a shave. But, following my philosophy, I walked up, introduced myself and asked him a couple friendly questions. Suddenly, out of the blue, he says to me, "Mister, all your orchids are dying 'cause you have them facing south. Too much sun, too much wind and rain blow in from the south." I raised my eyebrows. I had $500 worth of orchids on my property which were, in fact, dying, and no one at the garden shop had could help me.

I moved the orchids, and one month later they were springing back to life.

Let's be clear: Having an open mind and kicking "judgmentalism" to the curb doesn't mean that you have to like everyone. You won't. What you are achieving here is the realization that you are accurately assessing current situations, you are evaluating them on their own, without bringing the mental baggage of projected outcomes into play.

There is another huge benefit to approaching people with an open mind. As stated before, having an open mind allows you to tell another person how their behavior affects you, but now you realize that you cannot change them. You realize that perhaps they are caught in their own projected outcomes, and they haven't broken free. Rather than waste energy in the "rat hole," you can set your own boundaries. You have control of this — not of the actions and words of others.

Bottom line is we cannot change people; we can only discuss how their behavior affects us.

From there, we need to understand that it is up to that person to modify or make changes if they are willing for the sake of our friendship. After that discussion of boundaries, anything negative directed at you from that person should be viewed as not being about you. If you take it personally and allow that person to negatively affect you, it will close your mind and bring a reactionary stance. This is what we want to avoid.

Also, taking things personally will affect your openness to be more positive with other people and activities. Closed-mindedness can lead to assumptions versus reality and can drag you way out to sea.

Assuming is only going to get you as far as what you assume, then you come to a screeching halt.

A life raft can drift without a motor, but who knows where it will end up.

- Assuming that your message and or conversation is being understood by another is always a risk. Don't assume — ask the person to comment on what you said.
- Assuming that someone agrees with you and shares your philosophy can be disastrous. In the future you could be left wondering why they took a different path than the one you presented.
- Someone agreeing with your words could mean nothing. They might be thinking about what to

have for dinner and are not absorbing any of your communication.

- Assuming what the other person is thinking is like trying to rationalize with a fish. Don't assume, ask. Talk less and ask open-ended questions.

When I first went out to get a job, an interviewer assumed I was not prepared to take on the job because I was too quiet. After the interview, I called him back and in a diplomatic and forceful way attempted to increase my interview quotient. He did not ask questions and, therefore, I knew that he was not listening. He had assumed and reached a conclusion without an open mind. Within six months I was a top rep at his competitor, and his hiring days were over. Don't be that guy. Ask questions and find reality before you assume.

SURROUND YOURSELF WITH POSITIVE PEOPLE AND POSITIVE ENVIRONMENTS

Surround yourself with positive people who bring you up as opposed to bringing you down.

Remove yourself if the behavior from someone else is demeaning or not appropriate. This will allow you to flourish no matter what is in your past or what is directed toward you. It is important to have boundaries and be clear on what is reasonable behavior and what is not. Once you understand that the behavior is not an attack on you, but rather a projection from the other person, you can now more easily recognize poor behavior. Do not waste valuable energy trying to change someone. Remove yourself from the situation mentally and, if needed, physically.

Having a mentor is key. Once you discuss a problem, you cut it in half. Don't store negative thoughts and feelings. Share information that is to the betterment of each other so that all can feel good.

MARS

Mars is a planet that has been researched for a number of years in trying to identify two things: (1) Has there been life on the planet in the past? (2) Is there life on the planet now? The main scientific study takes into account the atmosphere, which is cold, thin, and dry and contains much less oxygen. The question is does the core conditions either support the possibility of life or reject it. Here is a good way to look at your surroundings. What evidence do you have that either supports your opportunity tc grow or works against you to grow? Important? Very! Why make your life more difficult than what it needs to be?

Your surroundings are mutually inclusive of peace, support, and happiness.

The same holds true for the opposite. So, with this analogy, understand that our surrounding environments — family, friends, and business associates — can either foster peace and growth or can take the oxygen right out of our life.

FISH TANK

Aquariums can be a nourishing or toxic environment for fish. A tank of brown water is a very bleak environment and the fish are up against it just trying to survive, never mind flourish. The fish can develop the fatal disease ***ick***

from this stressful environment. Soon they are covered in white spots and die.

Don't contract *ick* — identify the toxicities around you and detach yourself mentally and physically.

Do not be the shoulder for the continuous complainer. Be aware of the energy drainers that suck the life out of you before you have a chance to flourish. Then you can grow a productive peace of mind.

Further, do not be the shoulder for the continuous complainer. Live for yourself and give to others, but be aware of the energy drainers that suck the life out of you before you have a chance to spread your wings.

It's time for action... "Don't Settle for Less Than Success"

#9

DO YOU WANT TO LIVE YOUR LIFE OR LIVE SOMEONE ELSE'S?

Many of us are confused as to what is our vision. Even though we have hopes and dreams, we often settle for what I call negative evidence. Negative evidence can come from our thoughts and our deflated hopes. We often think, wish and even get overwhelmed with the possibilities of fulfillment, but seldom do we create the positive steps that will allow us to soar toward our greatest vision. Often we are overtaken by doses of indecision that lack direction and the inability to live our life on our terms versus what we think we should do, or what we think others want us to do.

***Stop* now, and think about the vision you would want professionally, personally, and physically.**

There is no right or wrong answer, only the world you want to create for yourself. My vision was to be financially successful and to teach my life lessons to others.

Understand that your vision will take accepting the victories and defeats as you practice moving closer to your goal. Be yourself and fear no judgment. Why worry about keeping up with The Joneses? Why cripple your vision to come into compliance with some perceived and accepted vision of others?

- Having an open mind allows you to embrace your life for yourself.

- We get caught up in pleasing others and we lose ourselves as to what we want and how we want to live.

- Most of us live in chaos or the chaos we let ourselves get caught up in.

Stop... The only person you can take care of is yourself and that means giving to yourself, treating yourself as your best friend, and doing the positive actions such as exercising, learning self-improvement, trying new activities. To create a healthy surrounding you have to practice being healthy to yourself ***first***. When you are healthy, you will start to see some people around you withdraw from you, which is good, because that tells you that they don't want a positive you. You will see others flock toward you and appreciate you and respect you and your time.

PRACTICE MAKING YOU THE PRIORITY

1. ***Practice listening to your gut feelings.*** What you feel is sometimes more important than logic. Sometimes you won't have all the necessary information to make a decision. Couple what facts you have with your gut intuition. Really listen to your gut. What is it telling you? **With an open mind you should now have better gut instinct. Go with it**.

2. ***Practice being different.*** The more different and independent you are the more people will be curious and start to initiate conversations with you. With knowledge comes creativity. With creativity comes diversity. And people will appreciate your ebb and flow in conversations and activities.

3. ***Practice doing what you want to do.*** When you have something that you want to do, or feel you should do, then do it, and make a practice of doing it. The more you start and continue an action (practice), the more you will give yourself a sense of purpose. Conversely, procrastination and inactivity will lead to self-inflicted stagnation. This might sound a little tricky, but, if at times

you don't want to be productive, listen to your brain. I personally have a bad habit of feeling guilty when I am not productive but at the same time I have realized over the years that this is what I want to do, and it helps me gather myself. Just don't let it become your means of knuckling under to fear.

Let me give you an example from animal brain studies. Researchers put a rat in a bag, held the rat tightly, and trimmed the rat's whiskers. This created tremendous stress on the rat. When the rat was put in water, it was in shock, stressed, and drowned. But if the researchers waited for a few minutes after trimming the rat's whiskers, letting the rat recover from the trauma of having his whiskers shaved, then the rat would swim for hours.

4. Practice being OK making mistakes. I can't emphasize this enough: Mistakes are a part of getting things right. Yes there are some mistakes we should not make, but if your intentions are good, then this is a part of your growth.

5. Practice living in freedom of YOUR choice. Live for your values — that is what gives us character. There is a difference between being self-centered and selfish versus living in the freedom of having self-choices. Once you make those choices you will feel the power and calm of knowing who you are.

6. ***Practice not putting on hold what you want.*** Life goes by fast and sometimes we are swept off course by currents when we are not actively steering ourselves toward our desired destination. If you decide to just tread water, then you might just end up treading water forever.

THE BIG LEBOWSKI

As we've noted, you cannot change anyone, you can only let others know how their behavior affects you; and then it is up to them to either want to make changes for themselves, or not. We can alert others to our objection to their behavior, but that is all. Any further action on our part is wasted energy, and harms our new open mind. So here is the most important thing to practice to make you the priority

Practice stop trying to control others.

This is an extremely important mental step, so be sure you are really absorbing this — even write it down!

After you have reached that mental step, any negativity directed at you from that person needs to be viewed as not being about you. If you continue to take it personally and allow that person to negatively affect you it will close your mind and bring a reactionary stance. It will affect your ability to be more positive with other people. Like everyone, I try to surround myself with positive people that bring me up as opposed to bringing me down. Perhaps unlike others, I physically remove myself if the behavior from someone else is demeaning, negative, or is impacting me in a manner that I do not condone. (It's my day. Why let someone wreck it?) This philosophy will allow you to flourish no matter what negativity is directed toward you.

No one is perfect, but it is important to have boundaries and be clear on what affects you and what is reasonable. We never want to run from situations unless it is necessary, but having an understanding of this core principal will keep you open to positive ways to view yourself and stop you from wasting time trying to change someone. Living by this principal will allow you to accept someone's decisions and not punish them for their own opinions, actions, or beliefs. And that, my friends, is having an open mind.

And there is a bonus! Practicing an open mind reduces intimidation from others. This is almost an accidental, but very important, result. Always remember: No one is better than you. Their actions at times can be more positive than yours but at other times yours will be more positive.

If you are intimidated by certain people, then interact with them more often, and practice breaking down your own walls.

If you fail with one person, move on to the next. If we open our minds by challenging our thoughts then we start to ebb and flow with an open mind, and the old reality becomes replaced by our new stronger perception of ourselves. We can give too much meaning to someone or a situation because we are uncomfortable or we don't feel in control. But do you always need to be in control? You are giving people power over you when they sense your uneasiness. When will they sense strength? When they feel your boundaries. Being aware of your own boundaries lets you project that strength to others.

#10

YOU'RE GOING PLACES

WHAT STANDS IN THE WAY OF YOUR VISION?

You have obtained a vision of what you want in *your* life. Your vision, not someone else's. But now obstacles rear their ugly head.

Often, negative projected outcomes will get in your way. Zingers will get in your way. Your resistance will get in your way. These will be explored in greater detail later, but for now, let's further define "projected outcomes," because until you can end these, you are stuck.

Projected outcomes are the result of our current actions ***and*** our past experiences. This combination leads us to being predisposed to an outcome tied to past negative experiences — before we even think or speak. It is simply impossible to be open-minded when we already have projected the outcome.

ARE YOU LIVING IN A NEGATIVE PROJECTED OUTCOME?

Below is a simple chart that allows you to see if you are living by the rules of a projected outcome.

Projected Outcome	Not Projected Outcome
This will happen	This may or may not happen
He or she always does that	No pre-expectations
Everyone always does that	No such thing exists
I can't	Might fail or succeed
I never have been able to before	Hey, it might work this time
I'm not good enough	I'm as good as anyone
I will get rejected	So what
I will lose	An action is better than no action
I won't have fun	Why won't I have fun

#11

BACK TO TIM MARSHALL: MY PROJECTED OUTCOME

My early life was predetermined. It had been predetermined since I was 6 years old and was handed a dump load of low self-esteem. To my utter embarrassment and horror I was held back in first grade. All of my friends went on to the second grade, but not me. I was little, had a late birthday, so the decision seemed an easy one. I imagine the meeting between my mother and Ms. Marble (my first-grade teacher) went something like this:

My mom, dressed in some beautiful outlandish outfit (she loved her clothes), enters the first grade classroom. Ms. Marble, weighing in at 300 pounds, immediately pounces. It was the middle '70s and my mother was young, pretty, and newly divorced — a sinful trifecta.

"He's just not performing like the other students," Ms. Marble proclaims a little too enthusiastically. Ms. Marble did love to take others down a notch. Opportunities to deflate a woman like my mother didn't come along every day. "You see," she coos intimately, "It's not just that he isn't on grade level, he's very distracted. The ability to concentrate does not exist in young Timothy. And, (the nail

in the coffin), he is very small after all. I don't think anyone will really notice that he should be in second grade..."

My mom, overwhelmed with three young children, doesn't know what hit her.

So, there you have it — the beginning of my projected outcome. I was stupid. I was easily distracted. I was small. My mind was closed, results predetermined by Ms. Marble's opinion of me in first grade. I would remain that way until I was 19.

PROJECTING OUR PROBLEMS ONTO OTHER PEOPLE

Another form of negative projection is projecting one's own thoughts and motivations onto someone else.

Sigmund Freud was all over this negative occurrence. This psychological projection, once again, is a defense mechanism that stops you from realizing a positive outcome. You basically dump your problems onto someone else, blaming them for your perceived projected outcome — even before it happens! We project our problems onto other people so it is their fault, not ours. And when the situation deteriorates, we have set ourselves up nicely to protect ourselves from internal blame.

Fortunately, you can overcome this form of negative projection.

The first step is to recognize it, which, now with your open mind, you should be able to do. Second, take responsibility for the projection, and bring it back home to you. Then really examine why you feel this way, why you act this way. Has it brought you poor outcomes previously? Do you keep repeating failing behaviors? Then practice stopping this thought process.

"The things we see are the same things that are within us. That is why so many people live such an unreal life. They take the images outside them for reality and never allow the world within to assert itself." —Hermann Hesse

I ran up against a negative projection when I was working for a company that was privately owned and profitable. I became successful, happy, had my own team, and was living the American Dream. Then in a meeting, the president of the company suddenly announced that he had sold the business to a major manufacturer. My first projection was total fear of change! My next was the projection of how these good feelings that were part of my employment would change.

My decision was to remain on, mostly from fear of the unknown, and hoping nothing would change. So, my projected outcome was limited. Then the dreaded changes started... But I decided to put my philosophy to work and embrace the changes rather than listen to my mind's projected outcome of "Ah, oh," this is all bad for me. And then the turnovers began.

But I became a sponge, embracing the new structure, learning something new from my new workmates. I built an empire of accounts from being relentless with my open-mindedness to learning new ideas coupled with my work ethic. There were some very tough times due to decisions that I did not agree with, but I also understood that I was not in charge. Things had changed. I didn't wallow back into my yesterdays and let negative projected outcomes take over.

I focused on the belief that how I handled the challenges would be my success or failure.

I also noted how many people left the company without even knowing if their job was in jeopardy or if they had a chance to excel with new ideas from a different leader.

Don't condemn a situation or blame others. Use your energy to create evidence of reality and then be true to yourself.

The employees who projected ahead out of fear of negative change, without having positive or negative evidence, failed or left. I began to see a pattern with employees who departed; they would also leave their next jobs on an average of two to four years, or would be dismissed. It is critical to come up with as many facts as possible before projecting ahead. Without the facts, negative projections can potentially create a lifetime pattern of inconsistencies — never giving yourself time to truly build on something new and allowing yourself to get stronger from the challenges and changes.

To change a career path out of fear could be the start of a pattern of self-sabotage or a sign of poor work ethic. Poor work effort creates fear.

USING EVIDENCE TO PROJECT POSITIVE OUTCOMES

Before I sold my company, I did the research on what purchasing company would be the best fit for me and for my employees so that our growth would still flourish as changes occurred. I wanted to make sure that the company I was exposing my employees to was a good fit and not just a release of head count. I took my time and looked deep into the executive team of the purchasing company and researched their growth and determined that they had a very strong executive team that was concerned with two things: integrity and growth.

Do the research or accept the fact that you don't want any control over your future.

Some employees were crippled with fear; thinking their job would change or that there would be some major hostile takeover. They began to show signs of immobility to the point that a few left without even finding out how the situation would benefit them. I sold my company and nothing changed except for significant growth and more opportunities. It is very important to know the facts first and build a concrete evidence list before projecting. Once the thoughts start coming on, without evidence to back them, you end up in bad places.

POSITIVE PROJECTION BACKED WITH EVIDENCE

My change began immediately following the sale of my company. The new company purchased a second struggling company in my same state, and I was appointed to run this company as well. This was another change for me that I could either project ahead or do the research and create a positive projection. I did the research, and I accepted that I had to address the fear of change that I had experienced and was now experiencing by an entirely new employee group. I didn't let it simmer —I addressed it just like I am addressing it in these pages. The transition went great and a fearless energy was created, immediately building momentum in a company that had struggled for a long period after losing its vibrant owner. The company was turned around immediately; the employees embraced the change from the beginning due to the evidence I presented to them of what the future could hold for them. I created their positive projection for them.

Addressing fears head-on can ease even the roughest transitions.

#12

ZINGERS AND NEGATIVE EVIDENCE DETECTIVE

"Distractions destroy action. If it's not moving you toward your purpose, leave it alone."—Jermaine Riley

As you grow in this new positive direction, your brain might try to stop you. After all, it has comfortably sat there for years controlling your life, keeping you "safe," and using your past negative experiences to steer clear of anything that might disrupt your little world, or threaten your long-held belief system. That is scary. And don't forget your fear of being judged negatively by others. You have concocted a way to keep yourself safe in a contained situation. It is time to break this cycle.

You are the creator of your belief system — ***you*** are the creator, not your best friend, not your husband, your boss, or your parents — it is all ***you***.

Why? Why are you right and they are wrong? You have value, you control your world.

Once you have opened your mind to this reality, you are on your way to a healthy, fantastic new mental lifestyle.

What stands in your way? Your projected outcome will get in your way. Your zingers will get in your way. What do you need to do? Hit those things on the head! Be the hammer and pound the negative feedback down. Once you start doing what you fear, your fears become less pronounced. The result? Confidence and an open mind.

Zingers are anxieties that suddenly appear and disrupt your focus.

It is one of the most consistent challenges, sidetracking our intentions when we are trying to achieve a goal. They can be internal or external. They can occur when you are studying, working, exercising or concentrating. An example: you are attending a meeting, invariably someone will come up, call out, disrupt, interrupt, text you or throw a fireball at you that has nothing to do with your goal or the meeting's goal. This literally can change your entire hour, day, week or even possibly your month. It's a lot harder to get back on course than to stay on course.

SO WHAT DO YOU DO WITH ZINGERS?

"No fear. No distractions. The ability to let that which does not matter truly slide." —Chuck Palahniuk

Make sure the external behavior that is being presented has to do with you! Most zingers that come our way are not about us, they are about someone else's character defects and come charging at you. If it is not about you, detach, and if it is something you have no control over, detach. Do not lose concentration on what you were focusing on. This takes practice, patience and understanding the difference between what you can and cannot control. Tom Brady is a master at this, and uses this phrase often.

Another example is a good golfer, who rids himself of all distractions and obstacles, and focuses on the desired outcome. Once you bite on a zinger, you just gave up time you will never have back.

Let me give you a weird parallel that might help define this. I'm a fish swimming along, against the current, because that way more tasty morsels flow by me. I am in control of satisfying my hunger. Unfortunately, I bite a damn delicious looking lure. The result? I'm hooked and being dragged on an unintended ride, way off my original course. And once I bit, there was no turning back. I have just taken a completely different path from my purposeful direction because I fell for that damn hook.

If I am driving and someone cuts me off, it can only be my decision on how I react. I can light up with rage, get into an altercation causing me to miss my destination, or realize that I have no control over the other driver's poor behavior. No one can make you mad. What makes you mad is how much meaning you give to the offending activity.

Controlling your emotions is one of the greatest gifts you can give yourself...and your health.

#13

OVERPOWERING ZINGERS WITH "SMOKE AND FIRE"

When a zinger happens, think of it as a small fire. Your emotions start to rise. You start to get hot. Your judgment gets clouded by the irritation of smoke. The fire begins to glow brighter. But you have access to two different hoses: one with water and one with gas.

You have a choice...pick one. You're the only person with that decision-making power. Are you going to create a blaze that is uncontrollable or are you going to put out the fire before it expands? The fire and smoke build in your brain, and if you don't make the smart decision, you will let the fire create the ashes of negativity and anger, which always leads to regret.

So, take a look at the zinger — where is the water hose? Is it simply that you need to communicate to someone that you will talk to them later? Is it a smile and a nod of recognition, listening patiently, and then focusing back on the task at hand? Is it spending a few minutes recognizing the zinger for what it is? Once you recognize it, you can decide, act, and end that fire.

Identify the triggers that upset you the most and why. Then go to the water hose.

Often, you know beforehand what is going to upset you, and if this occurs

often, then why act so surprised when it happens again?

Start being aware of what upsets you and try scaling down the emotions from a 10 to a 1. Internally measure and practice getting the lowest numbers and keep practicing. Use this exercise for any of the emotions you want to lessen. Have a mental picture of the water hose gently putting out the fire. The more you get a hold of your emotions, the more you will be in control of yourself, and not influenced by a zinger, be they self-inflicted or from outside forces.

Be in the audience of a play not in the play.

Will what you're about to say help the situation or hurt it? Being reactive flares the fire. Understanding and not trying to be understood is the fastest way to put out a fire.

Is what you're thinking beneficial to help your situation only? Is there a benefit to the other person as well? Are you thinking resolution or annihilation? The first one always prevails.

Is your pride now in control? We have instincts that push us to protect our image, but they cannot take charge. We have to be patient and not ignite the fire with pride. Humility allows the fire to burn out.

Sometimes it is gut-wrenching to say positive words when you feel violated; but you will not violate yourself when you speak and act kind.

ANGER NEVER WINS

"Anger is one letter short of danger."—Eleanor Roosevelt

Our thoughts are coming and going, and when we fight them, we add meaning and relevance to them that can build a small fire into a large one. Let your thoughts just flow without trying to stuff them. If you can give your thoughts a shape, then envision what it looks like. You will be able to replace the chaos with a positive image. Often our anger stems from feelings that we are being unfairly treated or just being violated.

We focus on what we don't want to think about, or what we don't want to have in our life, and we end up inflating the problem. Sometimes the best medicine is to change it up and do something that is the reverse of what you are thinking — such as complementing when you want to disparage someone or listening when you want to yell. Also, changing your physical position such as standing straight up, sitting up, standing on one leg, jogging in place or just physically being foolish; anything to redirect your thoughts for a period of time. This really works! The other option is just removing yourself entirely and doing something active like going to the gym, running, taking a walk — anything different than the situation that is creating the anger.

Sometimes we fiercely fight to be right and to be heard, and the only thing accomplished is that we have fed our ego. (Remember pride?) Our thoughts are just thoughts, unless you act out on them. So, keep it light and find the positive. This can be achieved by challenging yourself to a contest of reversing your anger to happiness by thinking or writing down what you are grateful for and how you can learn from this situation for the future. The more you practice this behavior the more you will be able to reverse resentments and anger.

Have fun with it because the only person taking yourself too seriously is *you*.

When trying to release anger, it is a good idea to write down your concerns and reach out to a friend or support person. When you discuss your anger with someone else you can potentially cut the problem in half. The more you become aware of tempering and releasing your emotions the less fear you will have in letting go of reactiveness, and the more you will embrace positive actions.

WHAT NOT TO DO WHEN TRYING TO RELEASE ANGER

Accept and be aware of your emotions; they are real and we are predisposed to fight or flight. You have the choice of adding gas or water to the fire.

Make a list with a water and gas column. Under the water column, ist the good you could do by putting the fire out. Under the gas column, write a list of how much worse it can be if you add the gas.

Adding gas is easy. Adding water takes work and control!

#14

STOPPING THE DOOM'S DAY NEGATIVE EVIDENCE DETECTIVES

How do we change in a positive way? It can be confusing ***and*** overwhelming. Negative is easy. Positive? That takes work. Why do we struggle? We have an alter ego who exists inside us to whom I refer as our "negative evidence detective." He is not like zingers, which are external forces. He is like a projected outcome, but more actively works inside your brain to stop your progress.

What is a negative evidence detective (let's call it "NED")? NED likes to think of himself as our best friend. He's our most loyal companion. NED is always looking at every situation, from ALL possibilities, to find that one chink; the one chink that will make whatever we try to accomplish, fail. NED saves us time! NED squirrels and forces his way into our hopes and dreams. He plants seeds of doubt, is a mass producer of black clouds, and otherwise creates quite the dark thunderstorm in our lives. NED keeps our hopes at bay. It's an altruistic task after all — having hopes could lead to disappointments. NED, like our projected outcome, keeps us closed! For all NED's best interests and good intentions to keep us comfortable, NED keeps us from turning our hopes into realities.

If you have a predetermined internal fail list such as having not achieved success in business, education or relationships, your actions will represent these NEDs.

How do you overcome this? You must prepare — remember practice? — beforehand. If I am going to chair a meeting, I am active in the planning, research, and communication ***prior*** to the event. Practice what you are going to do. Don't be shy about speaking into the air. NEDs will come out because we did not prepare ourselves appropriately for the task at hand. The NEDs take over knowing that they can take over —thriving on our weakness, poor planning, stagnation, which are all part of having a closed mind.

Open-mindedness is doing what you might fear.

And NEDs cause the fear. They label a situation to protect you, because previously you did not get your way, you heard drama from someone or you got hurt in some manner. To allow the NEDs with their past expectations to control your life closes your mind significantly.

You have to be aware and recognize negative thoughts when they emerge. You have to accept the good and bad as it comes along, but you don't have to sink your teeth into the bad.

As you start looking at small changes you want to make in yourself, *awareness* is the key word.

Be aware of the good, the bad, and the projected bad. If you don't get this, stop, and reread this section. Everything starts with being aware of patterns, thoughts, actions, immobility, fear, overwhelming thoughts, and those catastrophic projections.

If a relationship has failed or dwindled, or you feel that opportunities have slipped by, make a list of the behaviors that you created under the guise of NEDs. Be completely honest. Write a list with the cause and the effect. Now take a look at that list. Without the NEDs, what new behavior could you develop and practice permanently that would improve that list? What could you do differently if you could do it all over again? Studying this list, and acting on it, will allow you to review your past occurrences from an objective viewpoint and overcome NEDs.

And, all of this can be done in private — no mentor or well-meaning friend interfering and diverting us in our process.

Allow your past experiences to be stepping stones to growth and betterment.

Your past experiences can be used as a great resource to help you in your journey to an open mind. We can review what we did and how the outcome was shaped by good or bad actions and learn from these real-life experiences. It doesn't matter the initial outcome — you now have the opportunity to make a new current outcome.

THE DREADED DOMINO EFFECT

"If a problem is fixable, if a situation is such that you can do something about it, then there is no need to worry. If it's not fixable, then there is no help in worrying. There is no benefit in worrying whatsoever." — Dalai Lama XIV

If one or more areas of your life is under stress, build your greatness into other areas of your life. Don't let one area infect all others.

Some of us go through a breakup, personal challenges, a job crisis, or other stressful situations that can spread into other areas of our life. Our self-esteem can tumble, and our performance can diminish. The best thing you can do when some area of your life is bothering you is to take care of your other responsibilities, so the one area does not drag you down everywhere. If you choose to do positive actions when one pond of your life is a mess, this will bolster your other ponds.

Another way to look at this is being aware that you will be building a thicker skin as you take the bad, and excel in building the good at the same time. This does take awareness, practice, and constant positive action. If you keep moving forward you will see the problems that took you down will begin to diminish in their meaning and you will become more accepting of living life on life's terms.

Take on a research project, new hobby or something that can create positive excitement in your life. This will build your self-esteem.

"Everyone has a plan till they get punched in the face."

—Mike Tyson

When I started my company, I had several very big hurdles to overcome. The economy was at its worst, finance companies were pulling back or not lending, and my previous employer was using the fear of a lawsuit to stop me. I also had my personal life of raising kids, and various other responsibilities that seemed overwhelming. I stayed focused on building my company without letting the other areas of my life seep into that arena. I used the formula of positive activity to preserve and grow my self-esteem.

No matter what hit me, I challenged myself to stay focused. Any of those challenges could have easily taken me down.

***Action, Action, and Action* allowed me to look fear right between the eyes and move forward.**

Embracing the activity was so strong that I was profitable every single month and was recognized as one the fastest growing independent businesses in the U.S four years in a row. All because I did not allow the domino effect to take me down. I isolated and focused on the job and hand.

"I can accept failure. Everyone fails at something. But I can't accept not trying." —Michael Jordan

1. Be aware of what you can and can't control.

Fear will be released once you accept that some things you cannot control.

If you can control something that you are having an issue with then make an action plan and keep practicing toward a resolution. If you can't, then let it go.

2. Put more effort into other areas in which you can excel. One or two bad things ***should not*** wipe out your day. You can take a bad situation or something you cannot control, accept this, and then go after what you excel in with all the force you have. Keep your dominos far enough apart that they don't create a chain reaction.

3. Accept the negative. If you don't, then you will not know what the positive is.

We are not in quicksand. But sometimes when we start to sink the momentum that carries us down can create the quicksand effect. Pull yourself up to solid ground. It is yours. There is negative and positive to almost everything. If you don't accept the negative then it will be replaced with the positive.

4. Keep moving forward no matter what. Sometimes the distance we move cannot be seen and understood through our eyes. But if you always progressively move forward you will realize one day that you are creating a positive legacy.

5. **New actions create new moments.** There is no such thing as a bad moment unless you label it as one. Some moments are light and some are catastrophic, but we are in charge of taking over moments with positive actions.

6. **Don't feel like a victim.** Look in the mirror and ask yourself how this type of thinking is helping you? Your answer will determine your actions. Be a leader.

7. **Help others.** Maybe you can't smile, but if you make someone else smile then chances are you will.

8. **Strength is built on challenge.** Make it a competition with yourself and always try to win small victories.

9. **Don't fight your negative thoughts.** You will make them worse.

10. **Don't just say it. Do it.**

"Sometimes good things fall apart, so better things can fall together." —Jessica Howell

OPEN-MINDEDNESS WILL REDUCE THE WALLS OF RESISTANCE AND CHANGE

We have examined projected outcomes, zingers, and NEDs, all of which are holding you back and stopping you from changing our life and outcomes. Most change is a positive and not a negative. Embrace it. That is how we grow and get stronger.

Learning is at an optimum when change occurs and we *accept it.*

I have seen so many people run from change or resist change only to get caught in a circular movement that keeps them in the same spot without ever growing. New rules, new jobs, new relationships are all good if we embrace them. If we don't embrace change, then we are fighting against living in the moment. And we embrace change through having an open mind.

Having an open mind prevents flight or fight; running away from situations that could be healthy for growth, or resisting them. Fly and you will stay in your comfort zone and in the past. Fight and you will close your mind. Practice running toward what you know is best for you and what you want.

"If you don't go through life with an open mind, you will find a lot of closed doors." —Mark W. Perrett

An open mind is being interested in new ideas, concepts, arguments, beliefs, and the openness to try and act out on something that is new. A closed mind excludes new thoughts, ideas, beliefs, prejudices, and anything that could be perceived as facts from current and previous thoughts.

Open-minded people embrace being wrong, are free of illusions, don't mind what people think of them and question everything including themselves.

—Picturequotes.com

#15

PRACTICE BEING KIND AND OPEN-MINDED WHEN YOU FEEL YOUR WORST

It is the same philosophy as working out — it is the last couple of reps, when we are tired, that can strengthen us the most. Similarly with our self-control, when we are feeling our worst is when we learn the most.

Challenge yourself to constantly practice kindness, when you are the most vulnerable to stress, emotional pain or anger.

This is important: Practice being your best when you feel the worst. Keep on practicing no matter what. This will cut off your downhill snowball of self-pity and you will become strong and a positive influence on yourself and others.

Take driving a car: If we overturn the wheel, bad things can happen. But if we adjust to the ebb and flow of the traffic patterns — which are outside of our control — we flow nicely to a destination.

STEP UP TO THE PLATE OF KINDNESS

Imagine a baseball being thrown toward you at 100 mph. That is how we feel when we have to battle through flaring emotions. It might take many swings to hit the baseball, but eventually you're going to hit it. Just sticking the bat out over the plate will work sooner or later. You might be shivering at the possibility of the ball hitting you, but once you feel the baseball hit the bat you will experience a magical feeling. You will know now that it is possible to overcome emotions. And when the next baseball is thrown at you, it will feel like 90 mph, then 70 mph, and so forth. Your fear of getting hit is less because you are prepared.

Sometimes the ability to act the best when you feel the worst is just a matter of stepping up to the plate because you never know when you might connect for a home run.

KEEPING AN OPEN MIND

The beauty of practice is that you usually can do it anywhere — when you are walking, driving, eating, sitting, or at the gym. In fact, the only time you can't do it is when you are sleeping! Below are some simple practice ideas that you can do 24/7.

✓ ***Practice not expecting anything from anyone.*** Don't expect much from others. It will free your mind drastically;

and when others do things for you, you will brighten with thanks.

✓ ***Practice being humble.*** If someone does not embrace your humility, then embrace theirs.

✓ ***Practice being thankful.*** Look at past civilizations, or even some current ones today. Fighting for heat, food, safety, and living without medicine. Really, how bad is your day?

✓ ***Practice letting go of your past.*** Every positive action creates a positive memory

✓ ***Practice not judging another person.*** Or practice being perfect because you cannot have one without the other.

✓ ***Practice listening.*** Or practice interrupting yourself.

✓ ***Practice not putting yourself down.*** Or practice donating your time to help others.

✓ ***Practice letting go of what you cannot control.*** Or practice controlling an invisible car.

✓ ***Practice challenging yourself.*** Or practice letting others around you do better.

✓ ***Practice doing what you fear, only if it is positive.***

If it feels uncomfortable, then you are growing at that very moment. Remember: there is no competition or graduation.

#16

THE TIM MARSHALL BREAKTHROUGH TO BE OPEN-MINDED: BEATING MY NEDS

I previously referred to my breakthrough at age 19. My thoughts about myself were the same as they always were: I was too stupid and too distracted to do anything with my life. Like I said, my friends, my comrades, had ditched me. My claim to fame at that point — a growing beer gut. How I felt about myself hadn't changed. But I desperately and quietly wanted something different.

Looking back, that is the moment when I challenged my own NEDs. And it was scary. I challenged myself to do the uncomfortable! I tried something that my NEDs insisted screamed "failure." I knew I couldn't think myself out of this. My thinking had been projecting my outcomes for 13 years. With pen in hand, I wrote a list of goals that I wanted to accomplish. To begin achieving those goals, I decided that from that day forward I would not allow my cowardly thinking, commandeered by my NEDs, to steer my ship.

The first thing I did? I signed up at the community college. That action led to something wonderful. By just performing the action, something began to grow in me that I didn't recognize. I had the beginnings of self-confidence. For the first time in my life, I had taken control.

Signing up for college had gotten me out the door and on my way. I hadn't failed at signing up — and I had been accepted. A bonus for my mind! For the first time in my life, I believed I might be able to succeed. I was breaking down the wall of failure that I mentally had created inside myself.

I changed my actions and my thoughts followed.

Hopefully this story teaches you something else: When you feel things are tough, set small goals, take action, and take small victories.

Signing up for college doesn't sound like becoming president, but to my mind it was a victory that propelled me forward. I had accomplished something.

The smaller goals will keep you moving forward and soon the larger goals will be achieved.

Your goals will become bigger once your confidence opens up to the possibilities. There is no need for a long list of goals — in fact, it will discourage you. You will lose confidence looking at the list. It is good to have an end goal, but getting there can be a simple one-at-a-time smaller goals.

EVERYTHING THAT WE DO IN LIFE HAS TO DO WITH SELLING OURSELVES

"You have power over your mind, not outside events. Realize this and you will find strength." —Marcus Aurelius

The bottom line is that you cannot sell yourself unless you know what the heck you are selling. Making friends, earning money, finding a mate, getting a promotion, making a sale all involve how people perceive you—how you have sold yourself to them. This is not a bad connotation. It is reality.

I've mentioned that people will approach you differently when they know that you have boundaries and you have expressed those boundaries in some fashion. Now you are on a mission, free of projected outcomes, zingers, and NEDs.

What have you effectively done? You have defined the product—you! The more you are open-minded to learning, listening, and exposing yourself to new ideas, the clearer the definition of yourself will be to yourself and others.

Taking on more information allows you to clarify exactly who you are, your strengths, weaknesses, and interests. Trial and error is good. Don't be afraid of it—you have to challenge yourself in order to attain a definition of yourself and to create a path of where you want to go. This can bridge over into how you handle financial challenges, relationship challenges, career challenges, and student challenges. When you know what you want and who you are, idle time, weekends, retirement all can be defined better to enhance every moment in your life.

#17

SELF-MASTERY: A CALL TO "ACTION"

"Living in Yesterday"

"Learn from yesterday, live for today, hope for tomorrow. The important thing is not to stop questioning." —Albert Einstein

There are days I have a conversation with someone as they review the life they lived yesterday and project how it will play out today. My response to them: "Have a great yesterday." Yesterday is done, so get over it. If it rained yesterday, that does not mean it is going to rain today. If it was sunny yesterday, that does not mean it will be sunny today. You must take each day as an independent piece of time. Find the selling points of what you want to accomplish today.

Success is based on doing something you *want* to do, as opposed to what you have to do.

Some people have said to me: "But that means I can't hold fond memories and share them with others." That is not what I am saying. Keep the memories you like—and I bet you that they are positive memories where you followed the philosophy of an open mind!

SILENCE THE CROWD

If you are watching a tennis match and one of the players is thinking about a past defeat, it will affect their focus for today's event. Their drive to master the current moment will be disrupted, distracted, and end poorly. This is why it is so important to **practice positive activity** in the moment at hand. Your behavior will always follow your actions; support your behavior by feeding it positive and not negative actions.

"The universe doesn't give you what you ask for with your thoughts; it gives you what you demand with your actions." —Dr. Steve Maraboli

WHAT-IFS FROM YESTERDAY CREATE A LOST TODAY

Another issue that affects our call to action, and prolongs our being stuck in yesterdays, is laziness or complacency. This is a safety zone that we use to protect ourselves; sometimes without being aware of it. This allows the choice of least resistance to seem like the better option, but it destroys our freedom to potentially live out our greatest moments. The temptation also could be to replace negative thoughts and a lack of action with drinking, overeating, laziness, and isolation. Think about positive projection and you will create new actions and memories that will build a new future.

"When I do good, I feel good. When I do bad, I feel bad. That is my religion." —Abraham Lincoln

Life is not always fair, and complaining limits actions. Being a victim of yesterday's thoughts does you no good. When you have unresolved issues in your life, it will impact you negatively today.

You must take actions to move forward for today.

Always, and I mean always, look for ways to better yourself and be the better person. Work harder, and work smarter, if you want it bad enough. This will reduce the prolonged negative thoughts from the past.

PATTERNS

Patterns are developed from a lack of positive actions; being unhappy can be a pattern and changing this involves finding your truest interest. If you don't, you might be chasing the next great thing and never give yourself the chance to develop anything. These random ideas over time fill random voids of happiness, but when you do nothing, then unhappiness will fill the void.

Create a picture of your puzzle one piece at a time and practice creating pieces of your puzzle to fit your image.

"When we are no longer able to change a situation, we are challenged to change ourselves."

—Viktor E. Frankl

COMPOUNDING NEGATIVE

Thinking about what you want, but not planning how to get it, is a waste of time. Lack of planning, executing, and supporting an agenda can be catastrophic to living in the present. You can plan to be positive and happy as long as you follow your agenda with actions. If I schedule my days with exercise first thing in the morning followed by reading for 30 minutes five days a week, I am acting out my agenda.

FREE YOURSELF BY BECOMING AWARE

When you start becoming more aware and moving past "living in yesterday," that is the moment when you ask yourself what you need to do to initiate new activities and thoughts rather than pull from your old activities and thoughts. Another way to look at this is to consistently ask what would be the best way to grow and accomplish your agenda in life. Once you define what you want to strive for, you must practice this continuously because you can never move forward without having an honest awareness test of your accomplishment. The same holds true becoming more aware of what you could eliminate that is toxic or detrimental to your growth.

We must be careful not to live our lives under a layer of protection that was someone else's values when we were young, such as parents or caretakers, because you could be living in their past and not your present.

SACRIFICE

Activity and sacrifice can be exhilarating and should be viewed as boosters, like a rocket propelling into space. The thrust is exhilarating, and the force can keep the body locked against the seat, but the movement is fast and the reward will be immediate growth and new accomplishments. It is all a process, and to ignore the pain that gets us to any great achievement is to skip your stages of crawling walking, talking, playing and crying. All of life is embraceable if you choose it. So, sacrifice to get ahead, and keep practicing, but enjoy the sacrifice for it is part of your advancement.

SAYING NO

The fear of saying ***no*** can cripple you into losing yourself and living in yesterdays because you are not creating new memories for yourself, but rather for others. The damage here is huge—you could literally lose track of what you want in life. There is empowerment in giving, and the same goes for saying no, or letting others know what is acceptable and what is not.

Clear your own path in life without giving in to always cutting down someone else's trees for their path.

YOUR OWN RULES OF ENGAGEMENT

Develop your own rules of engagement. The best way to stay consistent and practice your greatest actions is by coming up with rules of engagement. They can be anything from avoiding swearing to acting out on positive behavior. If you practice your rules, before long you will have formed new habits that will be permanent.

Personal development is the ability to learn and grow from practiced discipline.

Development happens fastest when you are rewarded by others, or you reward yourself positively. To positively reinforce a behavior is to strengthen the probability that it will be repeated. When you reward yourself, or someone else, in a positive way you reinforce the likelihood that you or the person will react in the same way again.

#18

LOST IN POTENTIAL FROM NEGATIVE ACTION TO POSITIVE ACTION

"The true test of a champion is not whether he can triumph, but whether he can overcome obstacles."

—Garth Stein

THE ONE GORILLA THAT COULD BE HOLDING YOU BACK

When you have an open mind you are mentally strong!

Your mind isn't muddled with attacking another person's viewpoint. Your mind is clear. Your communication is clear. Open means space—space for logic, rational viewpoints, and objective conclusions. Somebody snaps at you? So what! You understand that the snapping isn't about you. You're not cluttered with NED! There are no inferences to draw from the snapping, no past evidence and hurts to attach to the other person's behavior. You have cleared your mind of the cobwebs of the past. When your mind is closed, it is reactive and subject to another person's judgments and perceptions.

What obstacles do you have that keep you from being open? Besides our foolish desire to keep NED entertained and holding on to our mental wall, indecision is a beast with which we must contend. What's wrong with indecision? Try to go through your front door when you're still deciding if you should. Did you get very far? Nope, you're still standing in the same place. Indecision is inaction. How do we change? How do we open? We become aware and we decide to take action. Otherwise we are lost in potential. I was seriously lost in my real potential for years. Let me explain.

The most wonderful people are successful people who have experienced hardship, challenge, loss, and unfairness. These people don't let their past interrupt their present moments. I have had some big challenges in my past, but I would not trade them or change them, because those challenges made me. People who have a colorful past are the greatest people from which to learn.

Those who have had the greatest challenges have had the greatest opportunities to grow.

No one has a bad past unless they believe it. Strength comes in awareness and acceptance; those two words build character. Embrace your past, good or bad, because it is just that: your past.

It is really hard to be open and consistent if you have a gorilla on your back everywhere you go. I know, I had a gorilla for so many years... I battled him week after week as his arms wrapped around my neck and clung to my back waiting to take over. Year after year, I fought the gorilla while striving to be the very best I could in my family, profession, and in my personal life. The gorilla was my drinking buddy on weekends. I could not wait until Friday night came. It was a given projected outcome: I would unload all of the intensity from the week and obliterate my mind. That was my reward. The problem was, the reward was a curse that brought me down and destroyed my mental consistency. Most of the time I would repeat the same celebration on Saturday to the point that my release of stress turned into a massive hangover on Sunday, where I had no personal freedom to do anything but recover. This brought depression on Monday, and remorse on Tuesday, and my mind started to feel better on Wednesday; by Friday, I was back to athletic conditioning to repeat the same process again. And each time I would do the same thing, because the projected outcome was always there. "This is what I do." Crazy.

I became aware of this roller coaster. I tried everything from personal development, yoga, goal setting, etc. Nothing worked until I became honest, truly honest, that this was a problem and nothing was going to change it until I accepted that I had a problem.

I opened my mind, and became aware of the hard truth that I had a weakness that I could not overcome. I had to accept 100 percent that I had a weekend binge problem, and the only way I could get the gorilla off my back was to admit defeat. I was successful, not an everyday drinker, and had a powerful outlook and message in my life. But I was so exhausted from the weight of this gorilla that I did what was so uncomfortable - I raised my hand publicly and said: "I am freeing my gorilla." I made new friends and created a lifestyle that was balanced with positive people, people who didn't drink and people who were "healthy drinkers." I embraced my sobriety with great openness, which brought me the support of so many.

Today, I cannot believe I wasted so many valuable weekends lost in my own potential.

I do not believe that we have to hit bottom to make a healthy change.

I was functioning, wealthy, married with a family, and successful. In my case, it was becoming aware of myself, becoming aware of my goals, becoming aware of the simple fact that I was not going to achieve all that I wanted in life, because four days a week I was in a fog. That's half my life!

I set the gorilla free, but didn't tie myself down to another negative gorilla—isolation, anger, loneliness. I built a different life, a positive, sober lifestyle that agreed with my goals and life desires. I would not trade a day in my life for anything other than cleanness and clarity. I accept that lots of people can have balance with drinking, and live in their potential without the roller coaster I lived. I truly had to put my pride aside, humble myself, ask for guidance, and listen. Sitting in a sober circle for the first time, to me, was the height of discomfort. I learned to understand that sometimes my negative or alcohol thoughts do not need to be acted out. I know these emotions will come on, but I also now know that they will pass—and positive thoughts and positive actions can replace them.

THE COMPLEMENTING ENVIRONMENT

When making new directional moves, and practicing our decisions, it is essential that you

build an environment that supports your new direction.

I find it ***extremely important to associate with the doers;*** the people who care and back up their caring with positive action. This is an absolute must for me. I will help those who need mentoring or nudging to move ahead or even those who need a total reboot to a fresh start. But if their drive is not honest, I will not put my energy toward them.

Watch out for wasting energy on people who don't care. Surround yourself with the positive doers that reinforce their actions with positive energy. We become our surroundings and sometimes it is important to take charge of your surrounds and customize your supporting cast to allow you to accelerate.

WHAT IS YOUR REALITY SHOW?

Would you have a renewed season? Does the same old episode repeat itself? Do you have some bad actors who bore the viewer?

Sometimes you need a new script or new actors in the supporting cast to create enthusiasm, excitement, and challenge.

We can get caught in our own reality show with a cast who hinder us. It is unfortunate, but true. Rewrite the script, or get new actors. The current script is probably cluttered with old memories that don't move us forward.

"Growth is painful. Change is painful. But nothing is as painful as staying stuck somewhere you don't belong." —Mandy Hale

Let's look at the difference between positive memories and negative ones. A negative memory can hold us back as a projected outcome, or have our NED (negative evidence detective) working overtime to protect us, not by our intentions but out of self-preservation. The result could be immobility and or a limited effort to move forward with replacing the NED with something positive. If fear is the motivator holding you back, then do what you fear as long as it is positive to creating good memories. It's uncomfortable, but that is how we grow—by doing what is uncomfortable. A positive memory is something that gives us a good feeling and energy.

When you break it down, a day is only a collection of moments that can be surrendered to either creating new positive moments/memories or negative ones.

Practicing positive actions provides the ability to achieve positive memories.

It is your choice.

FLOWING WITH YOUR POTENTIAL

Wouldn't it be great to live happily no matter what hits you; allowing yourself to constantly live in your potential? You do have a choice. Positive actions will always prevail, or at least shorten the lows, and prevent setbacks to your potential.

Embrace your life and understand that positive fear and frustrations are opportunities to replace the letdowns.

Always start with what you are grateful for and then engage in what you think could be holding you back. Those moments often are your greatest time to surge and grow. This also is achieved by writing a to-do list immediately when you feel the frustrations and challenges starting to mount. Tackle your list by starting with the most pressing challenges first, and cross off what you have addressed with action. You are trying to gain your potential.

Exercise, or some form of physical activity, will elevate your mood as well as create a goal that you can accomplish from the discipline of the act. Meanwhile, you are giving yourself a gift of increased happiness.

LACK OF ACTION CLOSES AND ELIMINATES OPPORTUNITIES

"You never know what results come of your action, but if you do nothing there will be no result."

—Mahatma Gandhi

Lack of action eliminating opportunities would seem like a no-brainer concept. If you don't do anything, you won't achieve anything. If you do a little, you will achieve a little. If you do a lot, you have the potential to achieve a lot. But how many of us don't act on this simple truth?

When I worked in a restaurant and felt sorry for my lost life, I was angry. I had been left behind. My anger blocked me from seeing opportunities. I had my walls, and I had NED, and I was in a rut.

When I took action, and made a decision, my life changed.

As I said previously, I decided to go to college. I entered that decision seeing the end game: a college graduate. Were there difficulties? Absolutely! I was a poor student, had checked out in the first grade, couldn't write, didn't know how to focus, and had nothing but 12 years of bad grades as a nagging NED, who I had to beat back daily. Though my physical body had finished high school, my brain had begun cutting off in first grade. I had a lot of catching up to do.

It took me three and a half years to get a two-year associate's degree, but I had challenged myself to do the uncomfortable, and I was not to be dissuaded. I was decisive. I was ***aware!*** I now had the controls. I didn't need to be first in the class. I would allow myself to be last in the class, as long as I got that degree. That would be a victory. Look at doctors. If there are 697 students in a graduating medical class, somebody has to be #649. But they all get a degree, just like the guy who hits #1. Doing the best you can is always the greatest accomplishment you can achieve, and not comparing yourself to others is the second best.

And don't let the excuse bug stop you. It will come at you from everywhere, but you have the power, you have the choice.

"Inaction breeds doubt and fear. Action breeds confidence and courage. If you want to conquer fear, do not sit home and think about it. Go out and get busy."

—Dale Carnegie

COMMON EXCUSES TO GIVE UP

- Did it once or twice and felt so uncomfortable
- Lost interest
- Never was what I really wanted
- Not worth it
- Too complicated
- I will never make it
- Too long to see rewards
- People are not accepting my change
- Too much going on right now

Move forward with new actions, or accept that your current situation is your desired reality. It is as simple as that. If you practice, you will create small victories and setbacks. Yes, setbacks! They are crucial to learning and moving forward. Embrace, accept, or own it.

✓ Act more, and you will learn more. Actions create momentum, and this will eliminate much of the second-guessing to create a greater will to tackle your challenges.

✓ **Have an activity plan for your task, and stick to it.** How can you achieve something without having a direction?

✓ Doing, and thinking about doing, is akin to having an invisible friend vs a real friend. There is no benefit.

✓ Activity drives the mind to adapt and learn. Activity creates constant growth.

"When your words back up your actions and your actions back up your words, sometimes the words motivate your actions and sometimes your actions motivate your words. Either way you are achieving."

—Tim Marshall

"When action collides with performance it can be breathtaking." —Muhammad Ali

You are the best in the world at what you do, and you aren't afraid to mention it at every possible moment. You're cocky, you're a loudmouth, you challenge authority, and even when you get beaten, you come back and defeat whomever beat you.

#19

ACTIVITY/ACTION

"Do you want to know who you are? Don't ask. Act! Action will delineate and define you."

—Thomas Jefferson

I often hear people say the same things over and over about activity. Today I went to Customer X. Great time. Good guys. They buy a lot of product. I think "REALLY??" It is like the clock striking 12 every day.

Here is what you need to understand about activity: Activity leads to achievement, but practicing and learning new tactics leads to success.

We are not robots, but most of us act like robots who are preprogrammed to act a certain way, and then are surprised when the results are the same or weak. That is not the goal. Static is not the goal, even if static is making you money. What made me successful in sales was not just the large amount of calls I made each day. What made me successful was that I learned to create conversations with strangers that I perfected to the point of building immediate credibility through trial and error.

Always be yourself with whatever you do in life. *Always*.

What you learn, and incorporate, will stick with you if you stay true to yourself.

Going back to my sales calls... I relentlessly made the calls, learning and practicing new strategies every step of the way, but most importantly I stayed true to me. I knew who I was through embracing the philosophies that I have already shared with you. I was not phony. I have taken that same practice with managing and running companies, and speaking to audiences:

Keep it simple, stay with your philosophy, and you will grow steadily and permanently into your potential self. Learn, embrace, practice, and success will follow.

One time, I sat at a desk for six straight days. It was a little rickety desk in the back of a warehouse with a big punch-button phone, a snarled cord, and a too-heavy handle. And for six straight days I made not one sale. Not one. Why? Because I kept repeating the same failed techniques, thinking that it was just a volume issue. "I needed to make more calls," I told myself. Because that was the easy answer.

Finally, I sat back and thought about what I was doing. I was doing what I thought every salesman is told to do, and it wasn't working. Why? I went back and analyzed as many calls as I could remember, trying to isolate the moment when the call had gone south. It was always the same answer—when I peppered the potential customer with the pros of my products. The very heart of my sales call! And it was disastrous. Right then and there I became aware of my problem through analyzing my past experiences—with an open mind. And then things turned around.

Practicing an open mind allows you to realize that positive activity will bring positive thoughts and behavior.

Remember that your activities, or lack thereof, will bring positive or negative thoughts. The more positive activities you do the more your mind will open to other things. A lack of positive activities will typically lead to judgment, and overthinking, and puts you in a close-minded position. Immobility and discouragement will follow.

Having an open mind allows you to live in the solution and not the problem.

Have a great yesterday. How can anyone move forward in life when we are caught up in yesterday's events or the fixed events of our past?

Having an open mind allows you to look at the positive. If you are negative you are probably close-minded, and anything new that arises will be directly or indirectly pushed aside and overlooked. Small-minded people are close-minded. Concentrate on what's positive and not what is negative. There could be eight out of 10 things that are good, but we can get caught up in the two negative things and have that be our focus.

Having an open mind allows for cleansing of stored negative thoughts, and allows us to act.

We can attach negative thoughts to us like a tattoo and attach the meaning of those negative thoughts to block ourselves from being open to new actions and changes in the way we live. Practice doing the opposite of your negative thoughts. Over time, this will build a pattern and absolutely will change your perception of yourself and your confidence in taking on new things.

Confidence is earned on a moment-by-moment basis. I don't agree with labeling someone confident or not confident. Continual action and practicing good habits build the confidence within ourselves. Yes, that confidence can become the norm, as opposed to self-discouragement or close-mindedness, but only if recent actions reinforce the confidence.

Preparation and action can never be overdone.

BUILDING YOUR TOOL KIT TO ACHIEVE

Let's discuss how to build a tool kit to help you practice by using this book. Treat this book as a living, breathing, person from whom you can glom information, education, and success. Don't think of this book as a demagogue preaching to you. Think of it as one human opening his brain and sharing his experiences for you to look around, and suck out every last nugget that helps you. Attack this book as something that should be shredded and digested—shredded by your mind and digested by your lifestyle.

"Design is a plan for arranging elements in such a way as best to accomplish a particular purpose."

—Charles Eames

- As you read this book, highlight certain points that resonate with you. Fill in the charts, fill in the questionnaires. They are all short for a reason.
- After you finish this book, page back through it and write down highlighted areas. Skim through areas that you did not highlight. This will accomplish two things: number one, you will reread the better points; and number two, you will begin to read faster and pick out the most relevant information.
- As you are going through the highlighted areas, write down key points on index cards, or if you are an electronic person, create electronic note cards.
- Start a fresh index card each time you start a section of the book.

- Once you finish, you will have a condensed version of what you read and you can use this as a cheat sheet.

- Now one last thing: Go through your index cards and pluck out categories that most apply to you—sales, wealth, communication, lack of open-mindedness, awareness, etc. Create a couple of cards that encapsulate what you most want to work on. Now glue that to your forehead. Just kidding. Read those two or three cards every morning.

- You can use this same system when listening to downloads, speakers, professors, etc.

Now, move beyond this book, and use the same method to create toolboxes for whatever you choose. Using the index card system, build an arsenal of topics in which you are interested.

To go back and find some nugget of information in a book or a lengthy presentation is difficult. But a year later, using this method, you can find it in minutes, plus you will actively welcome the information because you created it, and therefore you own it.

As you become more diverse and detailed in your learnings, you can practice teaching the finer points of what you have learned. Teaching will increase your understanding, and solidify your new habits. This is a permanent game-changer. This can work for financial objectives, career advancements, and any new trades. You can find the steps and the tools you need to take to get there by reading, taking short courses, subscribing to blogs, or joining special-interest groups.

USING YOUR TOOL KIT TO PLAN EXECUTION

"Vision without action is a daydream. Action without vision is a nightmare." —Japanese proverb

Too many of us lose focus on our activity plan as we get pulled in less productive directions by our zingers, NEDs, and resistance. This can happen quickly. You have to be mentally focused on your final image of success.

Motivate yourself by looking deep into your greatest interests or achievement desires. Prepare, plan, and ready yourself to accomplish now and in the future. Envision and write down what obstacles you will be crushing.

✓ Extensive research will limit the second-guessing because you will already have some expertise in your chosen area. You must create a tool kit.

✓ List your top 3 strengths and your top 3 weaknesses. Then take steps to build your foundation.

✓ The secret to consistent fulfillment is achieving something every day. Achieving something brings happiness, no matter how small or big. And this builds over time into a lifestyle of activity.

"Strategy without tactics is the slowest route to victory. Tactics without strategy is the noise before the defeat."—Sun Tzu

You have to embrace the tactics necessary to achieve your goals, and you have to have passion during this journey.

As an example, if you wanted to run for political office, you can't just be excited about the outcome of winning. You have tc embrace the efforts of running, and embrace every day as a new opportunity for advancement. The process or tactics, and the outcome have to match your desire, otherwise you could lose steam from lack of will to perform.

"Projects we have completed demonstrate what we know, future projects decide what we will learn."

—Dr. Mohsin Tiwana

The trick to completing a new plan is to set small goals to keep moving forward, especially in the beginning.

Keep your list of goals small and realistic so that they can be achieved.

The deeper you get into the project, the less chance you will quit. It is imperative to set your sights on small goals to overcome the quitting points that will rear their ugly heads. Most people give up on their plan within two months. Yes, two months. But if during that two months you recognize and enjoy small victories, you will knock those quitting points right back where they belong. As stated above, you have to embrace the process if you really want to achieve great things.

Always start with a purpose. Create a blueprint for your goals. Without a blueprint, you will lack purpose, which will cause a lack of actions and focus.

Act on the unknown. To create a comfort level and learning point you have to recognize what barriers you need to break through to make your plan work. This will include going through an uncomfortable learning process. But if you feel comfortable then you are not growing.

Constantly visualize what you want to achieve. The more you visualize your final image, the more you will create the steps needed for your plan to be realized. The visualization will actually create a desire for your brain to lock into these steps.

Create a positive vision and revel in it.

Maybe it's a dollar amount, travel, leadership or giving back to the community. What does this look like? What is the desired date of this occurrence? Paint your picture so clearly that you continually envision the reward throughout your efforts. This is the motivating force that makes you want to breathe the outcome so that nothing will stop you from achieving your image. You will embrace every challenge along the way as an opportunity to grow. Each of us is different, and your reward is personal, but you have to identify it!

Where does awareness come in? You must identify how your activity plan is fitting into your overall plan. This is where adjustments need to be made if necessary. Audit yourself and your plan: How is it going? Are you moving closer to your image? Are you flooded with new knowledge? Are you doing what's uncomfortable? Or are you getting complacent? Do you need to tweak the activity plan and work harder? Are you having fun? Are you open-minded? Are you conquering your fears? All the questions need to be answered to increase your odds of achieving. Also, learn from those who have gone down the path before you. You can't reinvent the wheel, just make the wheel a little bit better.

Be aware of complacency. Do not lose your focus. Look for anything that is getting in your way, including yourself, and address it immediately. Make your boundaries clear regarding what you will accept from yourself and what you won't. The same holds true for your surroundings. Do not let anyone, or anything, knock you off your path. No matter what happens in your life you need to breathe your plan just like the oxygen you take in! Be your own motivator and crush it with enthusiasm and fun.

Typically, positives will occur over time and in surges. Be prepared for regressions—they will happen and they will pass. Inspect the regression carefully to identify what exactly has occurred and why.

"By learning you will teach; by teaching you will learn." —Latin Proverb

Start teaching what you have learned. The reason behind this is you will be forced to retain more information along the way, and your teaching will bring questions directed toward you. Questions will open your mind up to issues that may not have occurred to you. By identifying and articulating what you have learned, you will give yourself more opportunities to learn and tweak your plan.

There are two important steps to take to own the information in this book. First, by transferring the material from the book to index cards (as explained in previous chapters), you are transferring the knowledge into your brain in an organic, dynamic manner. You are taking ownership of the material. Second, you are now explaining the information to others—teaching—and when you teach others, you are further impressing the information into your mind.

#20

IS FEAR STOPPING YOU FROM ACTION?

"I never worry about action, but only inaction."

—Winston Churchill

Fear affects your social and business life, hobbies, and family.

Let's look at fear: an unpleasant emotion caused by the belief that someone or something is dangerous, likely to cause pain, or is a threat to us. This is healthy fear—the fear that prevents us from harm and keeps us safe. Let's call this instinctual fear. We need to listen to this type of fear.

Now let's look at another type of fear, the fear that we inflate by giving too much meaning to past situations or experiences. This fear causes paralysis and limits our ability to move forward and to open our mind to the true possibilities of this day and this outcome. We create such a powerful internal challenge that we stay in our own head, not opening our mind to a different outcome.

The good news is that we can easily identify the past circumstance that led to the fear. Most of us know it, but don't dwell on it.

Most of us are intimated from pursuing our most important desires, because we hold this fear—the feeling that we are not good enough, or that we do not have the magical success trait that others have. The lack of achieving success is really the lack of opening your mind up to hard work, research, and accountability.

Having an open mind allows you to explore the root cause of your fear and doubt—typically there is little evidence behind that fear.

How do you know what you want in life or where you want to go if you are stuck in your past recycled thoughts and your same projected outcomes? Replace this with action steps to overtake that past belief. It takes a little courage, but you will be surprised at how little. We inflate fears, which can paralyze us. So, ask yourself some questions:

- What inflated fears do you hold on to? Why?
- What evidence do you have to back up this fear?

- What good does it do you?
- What can you do to learn about your fear and attack it head-on?
- What do you fear losing?

These are some questions to continually answer until your answers become so specific you can describe them in two minutes or less. Those two minutes can hold back your life.

Sometimes we bury our fears and then hide them behind pride, anger or addiction without even knowing it!

ADDRESSING YOUR INFLATED FEARS

Fear is part of being human, it will never go away. The more you learn about your fears the more you become aware of exactly what a specific fear is. Did you inflate your fear into something that was never that bad? Sometimes fear is only a perception that you created, and at the end of the day you are actually fighting your own misguided thoughts.

My first dramatic encounter with fear was when I endured my earliest panic attack in my college Quantitative Methods course. I was sitting in the front row not knowing, as I sat listening to the instructor, that within five minutes I would be rushing out the door in a desperate effort to find a phone to call an ambulance. My heart was racing uncontrollably, and as I waited for the wailing siren, I grimly thought I was such a young person to be dying from a heart attack.

I finally arrived at the hospital and waited to hear my last rites. I was surprised to hear the doctor say that there was nothing wrong with me... I thought he was crazy! I was dying and he did not believe me.

That was the start of a very tough battle with anxiety and panic attacks that had me literally running away from people. I did not want to die in front of them. My panic attacks followed me everywhere. Reduced to cowering in my home, I decided that living in front of a TV set was not a life, and I must do something. I researched panic attacks and started following the self-help advice I found on the Internet. It is probably how I first understood the importance of awareness and action.

Relentless education became empowering. Soon, I began overcoming the attacks, and enjoyed the feeling of success and achievement. I actually started welcoming the first signs of fear and panic; ready to go to war and hit the fears head-on, yearning for that wonderful feeling of success that would follow. As I learned more, I became more confident and the panic attacks were replaced with strength. Did they try to knock on my door to get back in? Absolutely, and I welcomed them in with open arms because I knew I could beat them. The attacks became diminished and weak under the barrage of my newfound knowledge.

"Thinking will not overcome fear but action will."

—W. Clement Stone

Inflated fear diminishes if you keep moving forward doing what is uncomfortable.

It takes courage to face something that is uncomfortable and new, but if you remove negative expectations by gaining the knowledge to defeat the fear, your discomfort will turn to enthusiasm. If you live in your fear, it will define your life.

Do not stop when you start to feel comfortable with some of the challenges that were previously uncomfortable. You will know then that you are good enough for success. Don't ever stop practicing. Achievement comes in surges and it takes practice to keep moving forward. So be aware that with self-analyzation you might get discouraged. Bottom line: There will be highs and lows; perhaps drastic ones in the beginning, but over time they will balance out if you don't give up or give in to emotional pain or discomfort.

GEORGE WASHINGTON

The turning point in the Revolutionary War could be the moment George Washington replaced the troops' fear with confidence. Until Washington took command, the Continental Army suffered one defeat after another, and the morale of the army was low. They feared defeat and failure, and the loss of their lives. Washington knew he needed a victory to reverse this psychology. He trained his men (practice) in specific drills. He gambled and decided to confront the fear. Washington crossed the Delaware River in a surprise attack on the British (action). The Continental Army killed more than two dozen British soldiers and captured 900 more, while only suffering two casualties (a victory, a stepping stone toward the goal). Confidence reigned, and the troops when on to more victories.

I am no George Washington, but the same rules apply.

I had a fear of rejection in sales, so I took on the action of cold-calling as many potential customers as I could possibly fit in a day. Painful? At first. The fear? Eroded and it was replaced with confidence.

My actions were just a form of practice. Call it practice getting your butt kicked, or whatever, but I kept on practicing.

I forced myself into situations that I perceived as guaranteeing rejection. Over time the rejection became less personal and I ascribed so much less negative meaning to it. I gained communication skills by my constant actions. I realized that losing that fear allowed me to be more genuine and open with people, which in turn led to more sales.

The takeaway from this was that my ability to overcome the fear of rejection catapulted me into being the number one account rep in the country. All because I tackled hitting fear head-on with an open mind and practiced. I did not worry about the outcome, I just kept on practicing.

INTIMIDATION IS A FORM OF FEAR

"Fear defeats more people than any other one thing in the world." —Ralph Waldo Emerson

How can you succeed today if you are stuck in past recycled and projected thoughts?

Most of us are intimated from pursuing our most important thoughts because we feel we are not good enough, or that we do not have what others have: some magical ability to achieve success.

"Ultimately we know deeply that the other side of every fear is freedom." —Marilyn Ferguson

NOT INITIATING A CHANGE FROM FEAR AND INTIMIDATION

Do any of these describe you?

- Not doing what you want, for fear of judgment
- Not doing what you want, for fear of comparison
- Not being yourself in a relationship
- Not acting, for fear of change
- Not acting, for fear of work

It all starts with change. Not initiating change starts with the desire to stay in our comfort zone due to fear of what change will bring. We could be drifting toward the abyss on a comfortable raft but we think we are safe on the raft. The shore might be beautiful and we desire to set foot on it. We could jump in and swim for the shore, but we get spooked and stay on the raft, floating directionless.

If you dream of a changed life, then I suggest you let go of the raft and start to work your way to the shore.

You might find the water only comes up to your waist and not over your head. And as you move forward with continual practice, your movement forward makes it less appealing to go back to your comfort zone and the directionless floating of that raft.

Doubt is really the lack of opening our mind up to hard work, research, and accountability. Having an open mind allows us to explore the root cause of our fear and doubt—typically there is little evidence behind that fear. We give fear so much meaning in our mind that we grow it into a mythical monster. You must slay this monster. Identify the past circumstance and thoughts that led you to the fear—***objectively***. Don't color it, look at it openly. Often, just doing this exercise will lessen the throttle hold it has on us. Then take action, and practice attacking the fear head-on.

I guarantee you will begin to feel comfortable with some of the challenges that were previously uncomfortable to you, or you shied away from due to doubt. At those moments, you will know that you are good enough for success. Don't ever stop practicing.

Achievement comes in surges and it takes practice to keep moving forward, no matter how small the steps.

There will be highs and lows...drastic ones in the beginning, but over time they will balance out if you don't give up or give in to emotional pain or discomfort.

As you move forward recognizing that you can, in fact, succeed, you can start to review your social, business, spiritual, and family life. You need to decide if you are settling or fulfilled in each of these areas. If you don't know, then progressively challenge yourself with improvements on each by doing research to better your experiences. You will start to see yourself growing out of some things and yearning for better opportunities. If you don't expose yourself to different approaches by continually practicing, you will just lay dormant in the same pattern.

Your main goal should be to find out what aspects of your life you want to audit and look to improve. Read, take short courses, subscribe to blogs or purchase books, and join special-interest groups, all with the objective of personal growth. With added knowledge comes added openness to change.

OVERWHELMED BY STRESS AND FEAR

Fears accelerate when your stress levels are the highest.

"It's not the load that breaks you down,

it's the way you carry it." —Lou Holtz

Be aware of your surroundings. We are exposed to so many different outlets from the media, from phones and electronic devices, that our minds are accumulating information constantly. We are more involved in more conversations than ever before in the history of civilization. As we pour more and more into our glass, we don't realize the glass is already full and has been full for a long time.

Charlie Brown's friend Linus goes from room to room holding his blanket as if his life depended on it. Wherever he goes the blanket goes with him—the soft comfort of having something so close and accessible, never putting it down. Our blanket is the cell phone. It finds its way into our every activity and situation. But the difference between the blanket and the cell phone is that the cell phone talks back. This keeps us on edge with every chime or lack thereof. We are inundated with information, mostly useless, and we are connected to that information and conversations constantly. This constant barrage takes us away from living in our moment. I believe in multitasking sometimes, but also understand that there is a time and place for everything.

Putting down your cell phone could be the biggest comfort you can give yourself, and the biggest opportunity to regroup.

It will allow you to focus on your moment and what you are trying to accomplish—instead of focusing on random information that might not affect your life.

FLIP THE COIN TO OVERCOME THE OVERLOAD

1. Be open to prioritizing the most important to the least. Some things are more pressing than others. You can get burned by not prioritizing and your stress will skyrocket.
2. Be open to making a to-do list of what you can and can't control and organize your day.
3. Tackle what you can control, from the most important to the least. With the list that you have

no control over, accept the situation for what it is and do not fight it. Let it run its course and you will let it go. Redirect your thinking to something that you can control.

4. Some people say not to multitask. I completely disagree. It can be fun and you can build your skills fast and become diversified. You will reach the point where you will be doing multiple things just as well as if you were focused on one thing.
5. Negative stress is created by trying to control something you cannot control and or not acting on something you can control. If you procrastinate, then accept that you will be negatively stressed.
6. If you feel someone is putting pressure on you, that is your issue not theirs.
7. Don't take life so seriously, if you do you will pass by the sunsets without ever noticing. We are humans, not army ants. Give your senses what they deserve...a break.

#21

FACE DOWN YOUR FEARS WITH EVIDENCE

"You gain strength, courage, and confidence by every experience in which you really stop and look fear in the face. You must do the thing which you think you cannot do." —Eleanor Roosevelt

Awareness and acceptance of a fear is crucial to overcoming and breaking through your barriers.

Sometimes fighting the fear in your mind will only intensify your fear and give it more power. In the seventh grade, I was rejected by the love of my young life—publicly. I asked her out, not knowing that other classmates could hear me. She didn't hesitate: "***No***, Tim." Red-faced, I turned to slink off and heard the snickers and laughter around me.

This one experience started years of living in fear of rejection. That moment became magnified in my brain: a haughty dismissal by a gorgeous damsel, roaring laughter, how dare I not know my low station in life, my stupidity. A brutal exaggerated hot mess in my memory. I stopped asking girls out, terrified of the projected rejection.

What I failed to realize is that if I asked out a number girls, more than likely I would receive a few yeses along the way. But my evidence was only based on one situation that my mind clamped onto resolutely. We can get caught in this trap, and never get out. I often hear someone say: "I tried that once and I will never do it again." There is a difference between risking body and limb, and making a lifetime decision never to try something twice. My God, we never would have discovered America or reached the moon with this philosophy.

Bullet point to you: The only person who is counting the fears is you.

You make the call if it is something that you want to overcome. If the answer is yes, realize that it takes a lot of evidence to solve a complicated fear, but sometimes only one piece of evidence to solve a simple fear.

HOW MUCH ELECTRICITY ARE YOU GIVING YOUR FEARS?

Plug in an electrical cord. Voila, power. That is exactly what you do when you feed your fears. They can overtake you and create immobility.

Courage is sometimes pulling the plug and becoming aware of what you can control and what you don't control. If you fear interest rates going up, you have to accept this fear, because you have no control over it. You could initiate an action to make more money, which gives you the feeling of control, but you have to accept your fear in this case.

Now you can identify your fear by either moving toward your fear and getting on the roller coaster, or accepting that your fear is not worth the stress and offloading it. If you wanted to write a novel but you feared that your story was not compelling enough, then you are creating a lost opportunity and a loss of a great way to learn and conquer your fears. It is pointless to project if the book will be good or bad. The most important part is that you took the time, initiated the action to do it, and the learning lesson will be there for the rest of your life.

CRUSH YOUR FEARS WITH SPEED AND ACTIVITY

The faster and harder you work, the less time you have to second-guess yourself —and less time you have for fear to take hold.

Speed builds momentum. Why? Because you have less time to question and second-guess yourself. Speed builds momentum and breaks down the wall of fear.

If you take on a project after you have done the research and calculated the ups and downs, press forward fast and methodically. You will give yourself less time to fall off course and the thought of giving up will be replaced with activity and momentum. The mundane task can be fun if you accelerate the speed to accomplish and tick them off your list.

Beware of the idea of the month... These ideas are good and initiate critical thinking, and often occur with many of us. Sometimes the idea could be a smashing success, but without research and actions, the idea of the month can accumulate like fruit that goes bad if it sits too long. Pick your plan, surge into the activity, and prepare yourself for the setbacks and the fear. Moving forward fast will allow you to learn, grow, and conquer your fears without nagging second-guessing.

Tennis and golf is based on practiced activity that builds memorized muscle movement to create perfection. The same holds true for mental activity, such as learning a new trade or prospecting in sales. I have achieved consistent results based on this formula. I am no more special than anyone else. But I practice hard, and work hard and fast.

It is the law of practice that turns the underachiever into an incredibly productive person.

Almost anything is possible if you practice hard, and fast and just keep going.

A little trick I learned to help me with this: time yourself. Timing myself was something that I took pride in. I would time how long it took me to close a deal from the moment I walked in the door until the handshake. This forced me to come with preparation, confidence, and a goal, and caused me to need clear communication. It made me learn faster, communicate better and handle objections efficiently. This is not for every situation. Some situations take time and deserve the process of properly uncovering and building relationships through useful dialog.

SPEED, SELF-EDUCATION, ORGANIZATION, ACTIVITY AND STRESS CRUSH HESITANCY AND FEAR

The faster you educate yourself on the tasks at hand, the more you will become decisive with your own decision-making abilities. This will build your skill set significantly as you work faster at multiple tasks. Your instincts will improve and your growth curve will increase to the point of being able to accomplish more, to take on more, and to control your own destiny. Ultimately, this will lead to less self-doubt and indecisiveness.

If you practice and go through the suggestions below, you will achieve greater results faster when coupled with a strong work ethic. The key is not to compromise the quality of your efforts. This is not about racing around with multiple responsibilities that result in sloppy results.

Successful habits will become a routine.

At that point your effectiveness will improve and your stress levels will lessen.

EXAMPLE OF SPEED ACTIVITIES

I would help support some of my customers by having speed meetings with their salesforce. I would achieve two things. One, I would improve my sales and management skills by practicing researching and speaking about a topic; and two, I would hope to improve their salesforce in the long run so their company sales would grow and ultimately I could sell them more of my equipment and services. No one likes a long meeting. They are under stress and need their time.

From the energy of the speed meetings, often I would boost their salesforce to a higher level in weeks, and the momentum would be contagious for me and them. This created a bond with my customers that would not be challenged.

This also is where you start to gain leadership qualities. You will build momentum, and your ability to retain information and lead will cause a major turning point in your life. People are under more stress with tasks, responsibilities, and pressures than ever before; that is why it is important to embrace the speed of your responsibilities.

The average burnout percentage is approximately one out of every three employees. Why is this? More demands, more accessibility (phones, email, text, and social media) to demands. Practice concentrating, and moving fast with the tasks at hand, in a methodical and purposeful way. Planning your time to answer or initiate random communications should be scheduled through your day at given times to prevent a loss of focus.

The activity has to be the driver of your focus, and the key is to get rid of the fat around the edges. In another words, go after the meat of the facts of what you need to accomplish. Subjectivity and drama can take you off your goals. Having strong and clear boundaries is important to staying focused.

The pace that we live in is often considered fast and chaotic. We either can fight it, endlessly complain, fear it, or accept it. Why fight the traffic? Practice flowing with it. Practice to the point of having your mind flow with the speed of the pace of your responsibilities. Enthusiasm is created by you, and by your own perception of what you regard as fulfilling in your actions or not. The secret ingredient to bolster your enthusiasm is to finish as much as you can with every task, goal or project. The processes must be embraced and used as a learning experience. If you start to compile too many unfinished tasks you can cripple the process of working fast. A reoccurring to-do list is a must. Cross off items as you complete every task, which will also give you a great sense of achievement and enthusiasm.

"You get credit for what you finish, not what you start."—Unknown

Prepare and practice, through trial and error, so the quality of your work does not suffer.

Practice with tasks that seem difficult; this will break you in faster, and the simpler tasks will become easier to complete.

Prepare and practice, through trial and error, those positive actions outside of your comfort zone. Practice with tasks and goals that seem difficult, because sometimes diving into the hardest challenges will bring out your best or your worst perceptions of yourself. Both are equally important. If something evokes the worst outcome in you, then that is where you start from, and what you take on next will seem less difficult. For example: I got in front of the camera at a studio and did multiple presentations without notes or scripts. I was told prior that I was not ready and I needed more training. I decided to do it anyway, breaking my own rules of practice. I was not comfortable at all. Disaster. But then I practiced, listened, learned. I built myself up from that experience and became the speaker I am today.

Relentlessly practice your strengths and weaknesses, because this is the greatest thing you can do. It will open your own internal doors. Breaking new barriers that improve your skills will launch you at a much faster pace and create a simplified task-oriented schedule.

The more you do to push yourself forward faster, the more the quality and quantity of responsibilities you take on will improve your chances for accomplishment. Quality in utilizing your time is key. So eliminating anything that is not useful will build your skills faster and sharpen your senses as you perfect your abilities.

A helpful way to stay focused is to break your day in two by achieving what you want by noon and starting over at 1 p.m. with a new agenda. This gives you the opportunity to accomplish in the morning and in the afternoon. And if your morning is ugly, you get to start fresh in the afternoon. Also, be specific with your time to answer text messages, emails, and return calls by slotting time aside during your day and not being constantly thrown off your agenda. Working fast effectively is about organizing your day and creating a flow of energy that is consistent.

To increase your communication speed, look for the bottom line so that you can get your message across succinctly and so others will understand your messages more clearly. This takes practice coupled with diplomacy and respect. Avoid energy-blasters and time-killers who take you out of your momentum.

Systematically prioritize your time so that you complete the most important tasks first. This will build a sense of control and achievement as you ebb and flow through your tasks and goals. Keep moving forward no matter what as long as what you're working toward aligns with your vision.

To give up, or give in, will only keep setting you back.

"It is common sense to take a method and try it. If it fails, admit it frankly and try another. But above all, try something."—Franklin D. Roosevelt

With any process, learning and executing fast and precisely requires learning the process at hand. That is why there is a long section on practice in this book. You can't understand the process unless you practice the activity of the process. Remember, there is no finish line, just a methodical journey that takes redundancy, with a gradual movement forward interspersed with surges.

MATCHING YOUR ACTION PLAN TO YOUR VISION

Build your day with related responsibilities, not opposite responsibilities. This will create effectiveness and better communication. It gives you the ability to redesign better approaches to similar tasks. For example, in sales I would keep my day consistent with either appointments or inside calls, not both. Momentum is created by redundancy and action.

Time yourself for tasks. Try to do as many tasks in one day as possible. The point is to get your mind accustomed to taking on many tasks to create **momentum**.

When you practice working faster your adrenaline will start kicking in, and you will start to feel the difference between negative stress and positive stress. Negative stress can be created by what you have control over, but you are not taking the action to control it. Guilt can set in. Or if you have no control over the outcome and do not relinquish control, this also can lead to negative stress. Accept that the efforts you put in will be your best and the outcome will be what it will be.

Positive stress is the ability to understand the necessary steps, and immerse yourself in the process. Your mind wars will be reduced and your resolve and peace of mind will start to rule your thoughts.

The bottom line is that when we don't do what we know we should be doing, or we just don't have the will to do what's uncomfortable, we self-pity ourselves to the point of victimization. You hold the golden key to unlock your own safe—if you practice the actions that you want.

Start somewhere, even if it is the smallest step.

We all had to crawl before we could walk.

AYRTON SENNA, THE GREATEST FORMULA ONE RACE CAR DRIVER OF ALL TIME: SPEED, PRACTICE, SELF-EDUCATION, ORGANIZATION, ACTIVITY

- Overcoming fear. His first Formula One race in Monaco is viewed as one of the greatest drives of all time. In 1984, the Monaco Grand Prix was held in a dangerous downpour. Multiple world champions spun out or hit the wall, but rookie Senna just drove and drove. He was gaining on his soon-to-be rival Alain Prost by several seconds a lap when Prost stopped his car on the track, protesting to the officials that the rain was too dangerous to drive in.

- Consistency. Senna is still the unmatched master of Monaco.

- He won on the streets of the principality six times. No active driver is anywhere near that.

- Strategy. Senna used to play chess with legendary team owner and master strategist Sir Frank Williams, and he would think five moves ahead. He was possibly the deepest thinker in the history of the sport. You could write an entire book on Senna's philosophical outlook.

- Practice. He could shift with either hand under immense pressure—before paddle shifters were invented.

- Relentless. Senna would rather crash than get passed.

- Sometimes he would put his car in a position where his opponent had two choices: let him pass, or crash. They let him pass.

- Desire meets passion. He described driving as a pursuit, and the surpassing of metaphysical limits. "On a given day, a given circumstance, you think you have a limit. And you then go for this limit and you touch this limit, and you think, 'Okay, this is the limit.' And so you touch this limit, something happens and you suddenly can go a little bit further. With your mind power, your determination, your instinct, and the experience as well, you can fly very high. [...] And suddenly I realized that I was no longer driving the car consciously. I was driving it by a kind of instinct, only I was in a different dimension."

- Fearless. Senna predicted someone would die in the exact place he died.

He went with a fellow driver to see what could be done in the name of safety at the Tamburello corner of the San Marino Grand Prix. He wanted to move the retaining wall back, but there was a river just behind it. Senna told Berger that he feared someone would die in that spot. Five years later, he did.

#22

DEFENSIVE PRIDE AND EGO: PART OF FEAR

"Pride will always be the longest distance between two people." —Kushandwizdom

Pride shuts down the ability to have a two-way conversation; and in the worst situations it can destroy relationships or careers.

When I hear someone speak or act on something I feel is a threat to me, my pride might close my mind to being open to something that could actually benefit me. I have seen people in the corporate world purposely oppose good solutions brought by another person or group of people based on their own pride. I have seen people sabotage and hurt other people's opportunities to grow within a company because of their pride.

Pride does not foster relationships; pride does not build character, it builds judgment. It is one of the worst behavioral characteristics and can cause our mind to be so closed that we incur self-inflicted pain that could last a lifetime. Sometimes being wrong is a lot better than convincing someone we are right. Pride in being responsible and genuine is noble, and is usually done through good intentions and actions, not through defensive pride.

Most of us are wired to protect our pride and hold it tight, which can be a strength if we use it toward positive actions, or it can be a negative response if we use it to protect insecurities and close-minded ways.

Your pride/ego has a picture that is often seen by others but not by ourselves.

It is very important to ask others, those that you trust, to describe what your pride looks like.

Ask how you affect them and what it is like for them to deal with your actions. Maybe it's being cold, close-minded, reactive or lacking in empathy toward others. Whatever it is, find out, because it could be holding you back.

"Ego" is the only requirement to destroy any relationship. So, be a bigger person, skip the "e" and let it "go"! —miraclessheep.com

How do you keep your ego in check? To answer this, you must understand that the people you encounter also have similar wants and needs. Most people want to be differentiated, and to be recognized as unique. So, the more you know about them, the more you will identify with them and the more you will find the balance in just being yourself. Your presentation of ego will be lessened as you let theirs grow comfortable with you. This goes back to again asking good questions.

Another ego inflator we hold is the fear of making mistakes or being wrong. We overcompensate for this. We judge others as well as talking down to others to put ourselves at a higher level. In fact, this defense becomes transparent to others. They recognize the weaknesses we are overcompensating for and our attempt to build ourselves up. Being human is to understand that there is no such thing as being perfect and the humility to understand ourselves and others develops relationships. Mistakes are necessary to growth and being wrong sometimes and admitting it can be a major strength and not a weakness.

"Pride is concerned with who is right. Humility is concerned with what is right." —Ezra T. Benson

PRIDE CAN LEAD TO SELF-DESTRUCTION

1. Closes two-way conversations into one verbal dictator. How can any one topic be discussed or problem solved without a two-way conversation that can create information for both sides to reach a mutually agreeable buy-in. If one is the dictator, then the other will be resentful.
2. Sabotages our business opportunities and relationships. It's hard to have an open mind when pride derails critical thinking and openness to good ideas or the recognition of bad ideas. One cannot hug the other person if the other person is not huggable. So how can one open their arms to give you an opportunity if you are so caught up in what you alone are thinking.
3. Inhibits personal growth. If you feel you have graduated, or know it all, you will stop personal growth.

PRIDE ELIMINATES

- Progress. It's hard to recognize progress if you are blinded by what you think you already know.
- Positive change. You will never be open to positive change if your pride stops you from having an open mind. Always look for better ways.

PRIDE AND RICHARD NIXON

"Frost vs. Nixon" reveals a man obsessed with what others think of him, the very definition of pride. Nixon always felt that others looked down on him. His defensive pride was such a powerful force in him, that even being president couldn't lessen its hold. In the famous interview, Nixon reveals his hubris in the famous line: "I'm saying that when the president does it, that means it's not illegal!" It is his lifetime of pride that culminates in that statement. His goals and dreams all are compromised by his pride. Eventually he acknowledges to David Frost what this pride has cost him, saying: "I let them down. I let down my friends, I let down my country, and worst of all I let down our system of government...and I'm going to have to carry that burden with me for the rest of my life." Nixon was impeached. That shows you just how powerfully destructive pride can be.

PRIDE HIDES BEHIND INSECURITIES

Accept that mistakes and being vulnerable are part of life.

Mistakes are necessary and so is your ability to keep moving forward. If you protect your pride, you will always be looking in from the outside and wondering why you do not fit. Be genuine and always practice being humble.

INFLATED RIGHTEOUSNESS

A puffed-up self will be seen through by others, and keep them distant.

FEAR OF LOSS

If you are always looking for new gains and building a positive surrounding environment, you will decrease the feelings of loss. If you limit yourself, you will fear the loss more greatly.

HOW TO REDUCE PRIDE AND EGO

Put your ego aside. Listen to those crossing your path, they might hold the key you've been looking for. —Quetzal

Talking less about yourself will open your mind to what others have to say.

This will produce an open line of communication that will lead to talking ***with*** the other person as opposed to talking ***at*** them. Think of a loud speaker overhead and you are forced to listen without the ability to respond. Do you want to communicate in that fashion?

Why do you communicate in that fashion? It is usually an attempt to impress another person and potentially the only person you will impress is yourself. The alternative would be to talk about yourself for ***the benefit*** of another. You can use your knowledge and experience as a reference point to give someone comfort and information versus bragging. If I am with a customer and I try to explain to them about my accomplishments, I need to be specific so that I am giving them information that helps them make their decision, not bombarding them with my successes.

Listen and digest. Try not to think about your response until the person is fully finished with their communication point. If you cut someone off with your response, what are you really doing? You are, once again, trying to impress them with your knowledge and smartness. This is a form of pride.

Stop and examine what you are about to say. Is it a benefit to you feeding your pride or a benefit of them? This is a great way to keep your pride in check.

Speaking poorly of others is a way to demonstrate your superiority to another. Ask yourself if what you are going to say brings value to someone or helps to build you up by putting someone else down.

The truest sense of a positive self and the release of ego is the removal of expectations. Speak or act based on independence and good will. If you act in expectation of something happening for your benefit, then you are going to be classified in the disappointment program. The disappointment program is always full of people waiting in line for what they think they are owed. The peace of mind and serenity of having a strong self, without a shield of pride, will be noticed and followed by others.

SOME SIMPLE TIPS

- Listen and talk less. It's amazing how much more can be accomplished when you listen.
- Say "we" as opposed to "I." Supports good feelings and togetherness. It is always good to have supporters.
- Wait for the incoming communication to finish.
- Don't pontificate, rather educate.
- Don't gossip or malign others.

#23

BACK TO ME: TIM MARSHALL AND INTIMIDATION

"You're not good enough."

During my last semester of college, my professor told me I was much too shy and I lacked presentation skills. For one week, I was very hesitant to speak to anyone, thinking I would blow the conversation. I started to get a complex. Then I said to myself: This is your negative projection dictating your actions, break the chain. You've done it before—do it again!

Several weeks later I was at a speaking seminar filled with hundreds of people and one speaker. After the speaker finished, I forced myself to do the unthinkable: I walked up to the stage and began to communicate with this glib man. I was very uncomfortable and my brain felt violated to its core, but I did it. And you know what? I survived. And I had a few pleasantries with the man.

I began practicing what I had just done. Forcing myself to speak with people, to people I wouldn't normally speak. And I got better and better at it. Sure it was uncomfortable, but do you think anyone talking to me thought about that? They were in their own world.

My next open-minded move was accepting an outside sales position.

This was even more uncomfortable because I had to cold call over the phone and in person. A piece of my brain laughed at me: "You, a salesperson ? Ha ha !" I was the least likely to survive in a business like this because I was so timid and shy, not to mention insecure. But I was going to practice.

Relentlessly I made calls on the phone and in person. At first, there were some very rude people, but I refused to allow their rudeness to enter my brain. Over time I started to get a handle on rudeness. I learned to communicate with the person as opposed to at them. I spoke to them with a sense of friendship, rather than purpose. And I started to appreciate the new relationships I was building.

With a little success, I began to practice calling on some of the hardest personalities and took chances calling on the highest-level personnel: presidents, COOs and CFOs. I learned how to communicate with everyone. I was not a rough sales guy. I was a genuine guy who cared, and learned how to communicate through practice. I was not the smartest and my product knowledge was weak, but I learned how to listen and communicate. I became the number one rated salesperson for a leading manufacture in North America. And that went on for the next 12 straight years. My communication skills, honed by practicing and putting myself into the discomfort zone, allowed me to hit some incredible numbers.

And it all started with an open mind.

USING AWARENESS AND YOUR NOW OPEN MIND

We become sheltered in a daily routine that closes our minds to what others are experiencing.

It's amazing how many times I travel to places and ask local people where to visit. I will usually get some scattered suggestions, but what is most surprising is that many people show no enthusiasm for, or knowledge of, their surroundings. We become sheltered in a daily routine that closes our minds to what others are experiencing. Get out there! Make a simple list of places that you drive by every day that have intrigued you, and visit them. Expand your reality and become aware of and join the world around you.

To show you how important awareness is, let me tell you this anecdote from my past life in sales. For the third time, I was sitting in front of a gentleman who owned a multi-million dollar company. His account would be worth $2,000 per month to me. His technology devices were outdated, but he said they "work fine. I just took this meeting cause you're a nice guy. I've already said 'no.'"

During the last two meetings, he hadn't wanted to hear about the better technology my company had to offer, the cost savings, and the increased office productivity. Nothing.

So, what did I do? Did I stay in my world, and keep hammering at him about improved technology? No. This time I went into his world.

I noticed on his wall an old Civil War pistol in a glass case, and beneath it there was an inscription from a Civil War battle. I asked him about the pistol. He excitedly told me its history, and where he had bought it. Obviously, he was a Civil War hobbyist.

Then I said: "Boy, the new technology of the Gatling gun certainly changed everything quite quickly, didn't it? The side that had it, won."

I saw the flicker in his eyes...and finally I had my connection. I had opened my mind to his reality, rather than dwelling inside my own reality.

Here is what the message is: **always relate to someone's world as opposed to your world.**

They will understand you because that is the world they live in—not yours. And you can't enter that world unless you are aware!

THE SAME OLD, SAME OLD...

Don't take this list harshly. Some of my friends have challenged me on this, pointing out that we all have personalities and we all have our core beliefs and values. These might dictate, for the positive, keeping some routines and habits the same for years. This list is for those of us who are questioning whether we have closed our minds, and are not open to new stimuli. If you are open, fine, if not, then this list will help you determine if you have, in fact, narrowed down your life and options, and are actually living in a "closed mind."

Watching the same type of TV shows

Wearing the same type of clothes

Having the same friends

Living in the same house

Never changing your furniture

Talking about the same topics

Always going to the same vacation spot

Listening to the same music

Eating the same foods

If you answered the majority of these questions with a yes, then ask yourself: Do I try new things? When is the last time I tried something out of my routine? Am I afraid?

#24

THE FEAR OF THE STUDENT AND THE STUDENT IN ALL OF US

"Education is the most powerful weapon we can use to change the world." —Nelson Mandela

Fear stops you from exploring the future and the endless possibilities available.

Why? What is the worst outcome? Failure? You are already at ground zero now. To not rid yourself of this fear cripples your entire life.

Most of us have gone through at least 15 years of schooling from kindergarten to high school - as well as college, and perhaps grad school. We just keep bumbling along. But how many of us have thoroughly researched our chosen field, or other fields, and matched up our interests to that career? My point is we have spent so many years in school but most of us never really explored the realities, and executed field research to truly find the perfect parallel to our core selves. Better to find out through research, than to find out through two decades of bumping along.

"The measure of intelligence is the ability to change."

—Albert Einstein

What am I going to do now? Most of us go through this seemingly overwhelming process. We feel that we are stumbling on, rather than having a goal in sight. We envy our peers who have known their goal since day one. We fear that we will, gulp, fail! That we will not reach life's starting line.

Well, you have control over your future—you just have to overcome the fear of starting your future. Then everything else will begin to fall in place. Sounds too simple? It's not. Just get started. Here are some great lyrics from Pink Floyd's "Time," that I always thought summed up this time in our lives:

Kicking around on a piece of ground in your home town

Waiting for someone or something to show you the way

Tired of lying in the sunshine staying home to watch the rain

You are young and life is long and there is time to kill today

And then one day you find ten years have got behind you

No one told you when to run, you missed the starting gun

"You have to go wholeheartedly into anything in order to achieve anything worth having."—Frank Lloyd Wright

First, build yourself up through your identity. Start with your name. Rehearse it, repeat it, and hold it strong. This is where you start now and this is where you started in this world. Now is your time to grow and build your identity in yourself through embracing you. Your name, your body, your hair color, your brain. That is you, good or bad. Embrace it and move forward from that platform. No one else is going to do it for you.

Your obstacles are only what you perceive them to be. **Your beginning point is your ability to look beyond the mirror, and create an image that is endless with potential.**

How do you do this?

Research successful achievers and the people who have bettered themselves, their lives and careers. Look at the people who have catapulted to success by creating their own opportunities. Also, be aware of those who fell into the abyss from not acting on their potential. Always ask questions of those around you, and look for what works and observe what does not work. Find mentors who can guide you and give you their experience, strength, and guidance. Go to free meetings and forums on a variety of subjects. If you already have an inkling of what interests you, even better. Don't hesitate to approach people—you will be amazed at their response to you. Everyone likes to think of themselves as an expert, and if you approach people as such, they will unload on you in a very positive fashion.

How you set your table in the beginning will sometimes determine what kind of food you will eat for the rest of your life. I cannot emphasize this more: Do the research, get out there, and expose yourself to different careers by researching fields that parallel your top interests.

Volunteer your time at companies, or be an observer whenever you are in a place of business, which really is everywhere. Interview business professionals, do research on the Internet, and study what it takes to be in a certain field, the positives and negatives. Read books on different trades. Take a career aptitude test and see if that leads you toward a career that you can envision yourself in.

Throw away fear. If you are poor in math but the aptitude test points you to architecture, don't let the fear of math stop you. Attack it.

Don't base any decision on what others expect from you.

My high school buddy was a total party animal, barely graduating, wandering through life. His parents insisted that he take an aptitude test when he finally finished college. His aptitude was for architecture. We all laughed. He didn't. Today he is an extremely successful architect who has designed award-winning communities.

Open yourself up to personal development that will allow you to build an amazing structure to affect how you communicate, understand, and problem-solve. Take the opportunity to be open to every resource you have including family, neighbors, etc. Live every moment with the understanding that you create your success and no one else does. The definition of success to me is doing what you love to do and growing with your life around it. Find what you love, and you can't do that without research.

With research and hard work, you will have a strong foundation to explode into the business world. Focus on what you can give to yourself and the company or entity your work for, versus focusing on what can be given to you.

Overachieving is accomplished by doing more than what is asked of you, as well as doing more research than is required.

Overall, it probably does not matter what career you choose, as long as you can embrace it.

Happiness will come from constant learning and positive action.

Acting toward your goals will result in self-satisfaction. There is no graduation, but knowing when you put your head on your pillow at night you know you did the best you could that day. Remember, if you look behind you, you won't see what's in front of you! Go kick ass and never look back.

Of course, there will be setbacks. But that is a good thing.

Setbacks make you aware that you are slipping away from an open mind—there is never any graduation.

If you didn't know what setbacks were, you wouldn't know what victories are. Take advantage of your setbacks.

"Life is a series of experiences, each one of which makes us bigger, even though sometimes it is hard to realize this. For the world was built to develop character, and we must learn that the setbacks and grieves which we endure help us in our marching onward." —Henry Ford

THE POSITIVES OF SETBACKS:

- ***Greatest and fastest time to learn.*** Embrace setbacks and don't fight them. The more setbacks you overcome, the greater your outcome will be.
- ***Greatest time to reflect.*** When we scratch our head and question why our ass was just handed to us, we begin to realize we don't have all the answers. It is time to research, regroup, improve, and move forward more focused than ever.

- ***Greatest time to try again.*** Just focus on your path ahead and practice and enjoy the process every step of the way. If you don't have fun, what is the purpose?
- ***Greatest time to make adjustments.*** If you look at any sports teams or businesses, they have to make adjustments to help them succeed. If they don't, then they fall behind. View adjustments as tweaks along the journey to your goal. This goes for relationships as well, make adjustments and create new energies.

MARK ZUCKERBERG

You do not need to have a diploma to achieve greatness. Look at Mark Zuckerberg. He had a vision, he did his research, he took action, and he succeeded. He is a perfect example of focusing on your goals. To him, college was a distraction, not part of his path. He focused on his legacy, not on what others consider the proper actions. He followed his gut. He fought back from failures and doubts. He won.

We'll just go ahead and say it: Facebook is the most relevant American contribution to the world in the past decade. If you disagree, name a greater one. Its creator managed to make billions despite dropping out of college, proving once again that you don't always need a degree to make it big in this country. In essence, he's given freedom of speech to the entire world. Some use it to make great political strides; others, to tell you they're at the gym.

The more you learn, the more you will understand that failures become a part of your success.

Once you have struggled, you never forget it. You hold the remote control and sometimes you have to go through many channels before you find what you want to watch.

"Don't let your fear of being judged stop you from asking for help when you need it…." —Jarofquotes.com

"Never become so much of an expert that you stop gaining expertise." —Denis Waitley

TO STUDENTS AND BEYOND

By now you have hopefully absorbed some lessons from this book. Below is a bullet list that might help you. I encourage you to embrace and practice them.

* Take on action. No matter where you start or how small the task or job is, dominate it and learn from it.

* Practice, practice, practice.

* Repetition and redundancy build the biggest winners or the biggest losers. It is the chosen action that is going to dictate success. Redundancy creates good or bad habits. It's your choice.

* Build momentum. When you feel the adrenaline from a small or large victory, don't ever stop.

* Always invest in yourself through research and knowledge gathering.

* Read 30 minutes a day. Nonfiction.

* Associate with leaders.

* ***Always*** practice your communication skills.

* If you worry about being judged, then practice making good decisions.

* The most powerful communication you can have is talking ***with*** someone, not ***at*** them.

* We grow in surges; usually during more uncomfortable situations. Don't go back to your comfort zone.

* In communications, always put yourself in the other person's shoes.

* The process is more important than the outcome.

* If you can describe what you want in life and business then get to work and do it.

*** Be the greatest movie ever made.**

* Expose yourself to as much as you can that is new and positive.

* Practice is a lifetime effort.

* Study and failure can be as important as study and success.

#25

DEBT, WEALTH, AND FEAR
YOU ARE A BUSINESS

All the information provided so far in this book is intended for you to open your life so that you can improve your skills by learning your trade, improve your relationships, and open up to new interests that will drive you to success. Now let's turn to wealth. Fortunately, you have built something by following the principals in this book: You are now a portfolio of value!

What determines your value? Let's be clear on this: only this moment in time. We are a moving target, and so are our challenges, victories, and defeats. You can have value in your actions but they change, and so will your life. We judge ourselves if we have achieved enough, if we are tall enough, young enough, old enough, smart enough. Having money, property, status, power, or conversely, no money, no power, no status does not matter. That is not what building wealth is about, unless you want to be constantly unsettled and insecure.

Building wealth is consistently riding momentum that leads to good action steps from constantly learning; that, in turn, will increase your value within your own outlook.

This will contribute to building your savings for freedom of choice, supporting your responsibilities, and striving for the greatest opportunities available. If we put too much value on a given situation, we are set up to fail. Let me explain.

When you attach something to yourself, eventually it will be detached and your value will be jeopardized. Maybe it's a job, school, status, relationship, title, retirement, etc. So, the key to building wealth starts with you, and how you embrace yourself. Your actions have to match what you are striving for, otherwise you will constantly be in a tug of war with yourself and comparing yourself with others. And comparing yourself to others is part of living with a closed mind.

If you live over your means and you fear debt; you miss out on the greatest gift you can give to yourself "peace of mind".

The very first step in building wealth is to spend less than you make. —Brian Koslow

Personal bankruptcies and foreclosures are occurring at alarming rates. Most people spend over their means. We are popping pills to deal with sleep problems, anxiety, and depression over money issues. Divorces often circle around the issues of money stress.

We make a tangled financial yarn ball as we go through life, trying to earn an income and straighten out our finances. What do we have to show for all the effort and countless hours of working? Once we do start saving, the next problem is how do we protect those savings?

If you have debt and feel you struggle with the stress of paying bills or no debt and are riding a wave of savings, both can lead to fear. You must become aware of how to face your fears of never getting ahead, fear of losing, or the fear of keeping your gains.

As with most things, to achieve the best analysis you have to detach yourself from your situation and view it as if you were looking at someone else's situation. Your job would be to list everything that the person spends money on, as well as alternative ways to create opportunities to save, invest, and increase their own value in themselves.

Remove your emotions and be aware of a want versus a need. Controlling debt is in your hands. Pretend you can rip off the waste/extra fat. It could be high interest rates, too many unnecessary expenses, a continued payment on a service you no longer need or use. Control or no control.

THE PATH TO OVERALL WEALTH MUST GO THROUGH YOUR SELF-DOUBT

Your value is determined by your consistent efforts, and actions to learn and create strength.

Below is a list I made myself a long time ago when I decided I wanted to be successful. The old saying: "The money will follow" is true. But in our case, we want to broaden this to "the wealth will follow." Our wealth is overall wealth that includes financial wealth.

Building wealth takes practice, but it does not have to be difficult.

First, describe the image of what you consider wealth to be. Think of it as pieces of a puzzle. Puzzle pieces are defined and put together over time to create the image on the outside of the box.

Create a ledger, and write everything that you want: a house, travel, savings, and anything else that you see in your picture or puzzle. Then write a one- to five-year goal next to each item. This is not about impressing anyone. This is about you and what you want and how much effort you will devote to putting your puzzle together. Your research, decisions, and actions will determine how the puzzle pieces fit together.

You are the only one accountable for your puzzle. It is OK if wealth is not that important because it's only important if you think it is!

What are the reasons for your puzzle? Make sure that your reasons are independent of what others think you should do or have. It is important to identify your deepest desires. You will tap into those on the road to success. It's your puzzle.

For me, I was not so concerned about how much money I was making, but how much research and knowledge I was giving to myself. The money came the more I increased my value as a person. I would budget and plan, but I was relentless in learning.

Money can be a measurement that can create a path to small victories. Have fun with it even if you start with a penny.

"Networking is an essential part of building wealth."

—Armstrong Williams

Ask really good questions from those who created wealth for themselves. You might be surprised that they are just like you.

Practicing is only useful if you have a plan. The same goes for wealth.

"The primary difference between rich people and poor people is how they handle fear." —Robert Kiyosaki

Do you fear your financial situation, even though you created it? Accept that you created it, and understand you control your ability to change it. If you are motivated to grow, and want to get past "getting by" financially, remove the blocks in your mind that prevent you from taking steps to control your wealth.

First and foremost, embrace it head-on. List two columns to differentiate between what your needs are versus what your wants are. Your needs column are your expenses, what you need to live.

Further, imagine paying everything in cash. This will change your perception of your basic needs and will give you a better value awareness. To see dollar bills going out the door versus credit card payments is quite a different experience. This will be an eye-opener.

When you isolate your needs, you then can take the opportunity to research the most cost effective way to cover these needs. Learning more on building wealth is crucial if you want to be financially independent. Books, downloads, classes, each can be a valuable tool. Financial freedom is earned over time with consistency and purposes.

"If you want to earn more, you have to learn more."

—Dennis Kimbro

Understand that your wealth wants ebb and flow with the changes that occur in your life. Be flexible and keep learning, coupled with working hard as you ebb and flow. Your money will be doing the same.

There is no age limit to building your wealth.

If you have to rebuild from a loss of savings, or if you are in debt now, then start immediately. There are people building wealth in their teenage years, and those who are building wealth into their 90s and 100s. You are the decision-maker and time-keeper, no one else.

Let's look at the number one wealth-builder: learning to sell yourself as a genuine confident person.

Speaking clearly and practicing communication goes hand in hand with wealth building, as do most of the strategies in this book. You create your own image and no one else does. Create your wealth image with integrity, confidence, and communication. Dress the part (without cost and ego involved) to create for yourself the image of success. If you look in the mirror and feel that image is one of success, you are on your way.

Take advantage of every opportunity to practice your communication skills so that when important occasions

arise, you will have the gift, the style, the sharpness, the clarity, and the emotions to affect other people.

—Jim Rohn

Be open to practicing your communication and social skills. All of life is selling yourself. No matter what the product or service, people buy from people.

Be genuine no matter what; and doors will open.

✓ Read, particularly information on your chosen field. This will build your actions into positive events so you will be armed with knowledge.

✓ Dreams don't accomplish anything. Repeated actions do. Don't be dumb. Inflated expectations will drive your dreams into disappointments. Becoming an NFL star at 48 is a nice dream, but tell me what actions will achieve this? Actions achieve the result, but the result has to be achievable.

✓ Don't complain about your circumstance, put the effort into bettering yourself. Personally, I sacrificed a lot of "play" time to build my second career. The payoff for me is that I get to write and speak and teach, and that gives me great joy.

✓ Think "small victories." It might take months of steady effort to start seeing "the big victory." But small victories will keep occurring. Think of them as runs in a baseball game. Each is important and should be enjoyed by you. Defeats will happen. View them as an out in a baseball game. Inevitable, but at the end of the game, somebody wins, and usually it is the team that has performed the most positive actions.

Move forward—growth happens in surges.

I hate to keep using baseball (I don't even like baseball!), but think of the surges as multiple runs in an inning. Small victories grouped together...

✓ Question experts. As you now know, someone is an expert at that given moment. That expert is one market or real-estate crash away from being an idiot. We are chasing the genius who is chasing the idiot. Be leery of fads. Be open, but be leery. When everyone rushes to one side of the boat, bad things happen.

And specifically on money:

- High interest rates are like throwing money into the fire Research alternative ways to get a lower rate. Don't feed the dragon, feed your family.
- Don't pay for fads and marketing. Look for solid merchandise that is sold with great discounts. Find them and stick with them.
- Be open to living beneath your means. Learn different ways to live the lifestyle you want. Make it fun, make it a game of keeping your costs down.
- Be open to owning your home or condo. Pre-payoff incrementally using the best and fastest way. This opens yourself up to personal freedom.
- Buy the ugliest (so cheapest) house in the best location. You will never lose.
- Be open to saving at least 10 percent of your income. Save some money each month!
- Save for a luxury, don't charge it. The saving process will become as inspiring as the luxury.

- Don't invest unless you are educated in your investment. Unless you truly are able to explain a stock market investment, don't invest. Identify the worst thing that can happen, and determine how much of your time and money you will lose and are OK with losing your time and money.

#26

BUT I DON'T HAVE TIME TO INVEST IN MYSELF!

"An investment in knowledge pays the best interest."

—Benjamin Franklin

If you have a typical 9-5 type of job, that leaves approximately four hours before going to bed and at least half an hour in the morning every day. Let's say you have nine spare hours on both Saturday and Sunday. You have roughly 40 hours a week that you can devote to research, learning, and changing your life. Even if you spend one quarter of that time—10 hours per week—think of the information that you can gather! **Make it happen.** In half a year, you will increase your knowledge ***significantly***, and open your mind to financial opportunities. In three years, you can double your income. What is stopping you? Inaction is stopping you. So act. Use the time now before this time becomes the future time. If you don't act on the here and now, then the future will become the present, and you will have no new future.

THE FEAR OF CAREER CHANGE

In the span of four years you can completely and successfully change your career. Or, in one day, you can change your career and then work toward success.

Once we pick a job or career, why is it stuck on us like a tattoo? If you are happy and fulfilled in your career, you are living with your values and are striving parallel with your wants and needs.

"If you don't build your dream, someone will hire you to help build theirs." —Tony Gaskins

If you are not happy and want to change careers, do it. Maybe the learning curve is six months, or maybe you have to go back to school, but is anything worse than not enjoying your work life? Maybe you start a new profession at age 40 that will last until your 75. Age is the number one thing that is irrelevant (unless you have to tackle people for a living). My point is how much time are you really giving up to learn something new? Maybe you take classes on the weekend, or twice a week, and slowly transition yourself. The more you learn and grow the more you can choose the pieces for a new puzzle. Do something completely different if you prefer; whatever it is, you will have nothing to lose by learning a new trade or getting back to studying.

Worst-case scenario is that you become more educated, and that always leads to a positive.

"The secret of change is to focus all of your energy not on fight the old, but on building the new."—Socrates

Who says you have to be stuck? You are the only decision-maker. If you are a tow truck driver at 22, by the time you are 37 you could be a brain surgeon. Or if you want to be an attorney, maybe you start practicing law when you're 35. The career shifts could be a six-month learning curve, or it could be a multi-level learning curve of up to 15 years. If you have the interest and that's what you want out of your life, then make a plan and start somewhere and never stop. ***Why not you? Why not new?*** **Why not now?**

How do people expect me to choose a career path at 16; I can't even choose what I want for dinner.—Anonymous

#27

GROWTH VS. FEAR

Business owners create financial security and stress for themselves, and jobs for others. It takes a lot of courage and fortitude to start something. I have been there and it is not easy. But when you succeed you will feel so fulfilled and happy that you will want to start all over again!

When starting your own company, be prepared for the unexpected, to be frazzled, to have sleepless nights and to work in the front lines.

Relationships, Quality, and Margins are everything.

Starting a business begins with knowledge. From reading this book, you hopefully have carved out a successful method of gaining all the knowledge that you will need, and you have gained knowledge that parallels your interest in starting a business. Start making contacts with people who are in similar businesses, but not your geographic competitors. If you threaten their marketplace, why would they help you? When I started my company, I researched every bit of available information. I traveled out of state to talk to similar business owners who would never be my competitors. I stopped my pre-launch research when

I reached the point that I knew more than the business owner across the table from me. Anything is possible if you learn the strengths, weaknesses, opportunities, and threats of your proposed business.

Learn the struggles of similar companies from the biggest to the smallest. If you are a control freak, then you ***must*** get a partner who is not.

You cannot control everything; you only can attempt to control the result.

Focus on your goal. Focus on your desired result. Control freaks can get lost in the minutiae, and miss the big opportunity. Control freaks are prone to being distracted by zingers, and just like the fish that bit the lure, get dragged off in the wrong direction.

I used the advice I am giving you, and I grew from a desk and telephone into one of the most competitive office technology businesses in America. I was profitable from month one until the day I sold my business. My number one secret was that I was in the front lines **and never stepped back.** I learned to never hire an employee until it was more than a necessity—when it would hurt business growth ***not*** to hire. As my company grew I started hiring people who had the skill set to work independently, but I always inspected the final result. Always.

KNOW YOUR STORY

"If you keep telling the same sad story, you will keep living the same sad small life."—Jean Houston

"Lastly get emotionally connected to your story so you can deliver it. You know if you can't deliver the emotions to your script there's no point to your story."

—Robert Redford

When I meet with people, the first thing I ask them is: What is your story? Everyone has a personal story filled with different exposures that are unique. Often they are shy and are not aware that their achievements or struggles; or their trying times are colorful, interesting, and full of growth. Those who have struggled, or have been challenged, have the most to show us.

Your story is you.

If you cannot convey your story, you lessen yourself in your eyes and in others' eyes.

Create your story based on your experiences, strengths, and weaknesses. This is what you walk with and talk with. It is your essence. Be proud no matter what, and understand your mistakes are only opportunities to grow and give more. The power and essence of who you are has to be instilled in your foundation.

Be proud of it! No matter what! If you struggle with this concept, then be relentless with positive action until you have another story. No one else is responsible for this, and the ball is in your court now and always. What you do with it is your choice so ***accept*** your life, and love it or make changes so you can embrace it. Remember this: ***Accept it and love it, or address it and change it!***

BUILD YOUR REPUTATION

"It takes 20 years to build a reputation and five minutes to ruin it.

If you think about that, you'll do things differently."

—Warren Buffett

Continuously practice positive activity.

Your reputation is yours to build, protect and create into a legacy. Achievement is based on what you say and how you lead yourself. Be kind and genuine, but deliver on what you say you will do; overdeliver when you can. Caring for others is key, and is only useful when you actually do care. You cannot pretend to give to others. This will only create resentment inside of you, and you will always expect to get something back. Expectations are the perpetrator of resentments. That is why it is so important not to judge, and to ask good questions when you interact. You will find that most people are extremely kind and are looking for kindness and trust in return. Once you earn someone's trust you will be powerful in their eyes. This is never to be taken for granted. Burn a bridge and fear will follow over your shoulder. The better actions you make, the more people will come to you, and the more you will control your life and your peace of mind. Your reputation will remain intact. People follow those who create evidence through action and energy.

Your words can hurt or heal, and your actions can lead or destroy.

It is your choice.

IDENTIFY AND LIVE BY YOUR PERSONAL MOTTO

"Work for a cause, not for applause. Live life to express, not to impress. Don't strive to make your presence noticed, just make your absence felt." —Unknown

Now you should be able to identify a personal motto. A company has a mission statement, which is really a motto. You should too.

A personal motto is having a practiced behavior that you choose to live throughout your life. My personal motto is that I always better myself to ensure I communicate in a way that builds integrity and humility in myself, and hopefully teaches others through my actions.

BE YOUR OWN BOSS

"Have the courage to follow your heart and intuition. They somehow know what you truly want to become."

—Steve Jobs

The harder you work, the more you will create your own freedom. From the very first day I started my job, until I sold my own multimillion-dollar company, my own competition with myself was my own biggest driver. I didn't compete against others or try to beat others. I constantly improved my skills and set the bar higher for myself, even with many management and leadership philosophy changes. I listened to my intuition, took action, management noticed my self-motivation, and I enjoyed my freedom. As I have repeated to you often,

it is about practicing your actions.

Start, build, and you will find yourself surging into your days. And ***always*** start your day by reading for 30 minutes on a life skill that applies to your expertise. It works!

OPRAH WINFREY AND STEVEN SPIELBERG

Overcoming an abusive household, Oprah is the epitome of a strong, independent, woman who took action and followed her dream. Now she has achieved a television show, book club, magazine, and a television network. At

61, she's worth more than $3 billion, and is considered one of the most influential people of the decade.

Steven Spielberg was rejected twice from USC film school.

"Never become so much of an expert that you stop gaining expertise. View life as a continuous learning experience." —Denis Waitley

Learn from those who know best, and who have achieved results through actions.

You don't need to re-create the wheel, just create a better wheel.

And don't give up—deep-rooted action will lead you forward. Look for this in a mentor and follow their example.

DESIGN YOUR BUSINESS AND PERSONAL PLAN

Our journey through this book is winding down. You now have the mental approach to succeed. You have a roadmap to success.

And **you understand that your fears cannot stop you.** Below is some advice that you will have found elsewhere in this book, but it is time to gather it together in one place. Please study this. The launch of your business depends upon it.

- Research every bit of your personal business plan. Start with yourself as the business.
- Your identity has to be clearly formed first. Give yourself every opportunity to grow. Define your vision. Write down the actions needed to achieve your vision. Identify why the sacrifices are worth the effort to create a positive attitude. If your attitude is good then good things happen. Then do the research.
- Beware of complacency. If you begin to fall into this, question how bad you want to support your vision. Do you really want this vision? It is important to understand that your vision could change to more closely align with your true self. Every time you align more closely with your true self and true goal, your rate of success advances.
- Urgency is a key. Accelerate your actions to end too much second-guessing. This does not mean

to blindly go forward, but rather to be relentless in your research to support your vision. Be focused on being specific on your plan. Give yourself deadlines and a schedule to follow.

"Planning is bringing the future into the present so you can do something about it now." —Alan Lakein

- You have to be the best salesperson, even if you are having a bad day. You are your own boss no matter what. You can run your own life/company with vigor and enthusiasm or you can be controlled by forces, internal and external, that are dragging you around. Focus on the puzzle and be your greatest salesperson no matter what. This takes relentless practice, especially if your day or your mood for the day is not good. We are all in sales some way or another and the more we believe in our strengths the more we accomplish and discard the baggage.
- Run lean. Be your own auditor and apply benchmarks. Benchmarks are mathematical numbers generated by your expenses versus what you are gaining. You

cannot live in peace if these are not positive. You can create your own benchmarks in your savings, expenses, and overall living plan.

- Love your customers and show it. The more you give, the more you get. Being genuine and caring to your customers, family, and friends above your own needs will promote trust and success.
- Avoid debt as much as possible. Debt lowers your future standard of living and causes negative stress. Build assets one at a time. Your lodging is a priority.
- Attack problems, do not delay. The faster you hit the problems head-on, the less likely the problems will take you down over time.
- Open-mindedness and drive always trump talent. Clear your path with open- minded drive and you will learn to always fight fear with action.
- Teach, delegate, and inspect. Learn first, trust second, and inspire third.
- Choose employees, friends, and support groups that are in parallel to your vision.

- ALWAYS lead by example. Otherwise, you will follow someone else's vision not yours. Enthusiasm is contagious.

Fear arises, and a downfall can occur, if we put too much value in one given situation. When you attach something to yourself, eventually it will be detached and your value will be jeopardized. Maybe it's a job, school or social status, or a relationship.

The key to building wealth starts with you and how you embrace yourself, grow, and accept that changes are a part of life.

What you do with changes will build or hurt your legacy.

Start small so that you can get to know every detail of your business, so as you grow you will know how to manage and direct from your own hands-on experience. Teach, delegate, and ***always*** inspect. The people who do this grow and grow big. I personally had to learn this process the hard way. But fortunately for me, the business model that my research had exposed was undeniable, and I was successful.

If possible, stay away from creating debt, but if you must create debt, make sure that you have a Plan B to pay off the debt if your business model does not work. Do not reinvent the wheel, stick with business models that, from your research, you know will work. You have gathered the research for months, you have great knowledge of the business climate, now you must act relentlessly.

Make your business a little bit better than the competition, then make it a lot better. You can put your new skills of communications and your open mind to work for you. Stake out your territory, and fight to retain it. ***And keep reading.*** It is death to stop gaining more knowledge. All businesses and industries change, but through your research you will be aware of these changes, and you now approach change as opportunity, and you will be able to take advantage of them.

Don't get greedy. Entrepreneurs are the core of the economy, and they should be respected as long as the core value and integrity of the business is retained. How many restaurants have you seen start out great, and then dwindle into bankruptcy as the owner first gets rich, then gets lazy and wanders from the business' founding principles.

Here is a simple question to keep asking yourself as you grow your business: Am I changing this for the betterment of my wealth, or the betterment of serving my customers? If it is for the betterment of other people as a whole, and not just the betterment of your wealth, then you are on the right path. If your "growth" or change is really a disguise to take other people's hard-earned cash, you will lose.

When I sat down with Bernie Marcus, founder of Home Depot, his most important rule was, "take care and love your customers." When he opened his first store he went out of his way to greet every single customer. As he said: "People buy from people." Even with today's technologies and electronic shopping, people are still buying from people, and they always will. When you receive a product you ordered online that is less than described by the company, who do you get mad at? A generic company, or a person or people? You get mad at people. Think about it. You conjure up an image of a person or some group of people gathered together for the purpose of ripping you off. You don't get angry at some faceless company.

Mastery of a company is knowing your company like it was you. If you are not the greatest salesperson for your company, then you will fail. If you are not the greatest salesperson for your company, then something is very wrong, and you should pull the plug on the company immediately. It starts and ends with you. If you can't sell your company's worth, you do not believe in your company's worth, and that will haunt the company into an early grave.

#28

FEAR OF MATH

To be in charge of your life, you have to know math. For some of us this is daunting. But you have to attack this with the same open mind that you developed to improve your speech. You don't need to be at a NASA level, you just need some basics.

Math can build your wealth fortress, or destroy it.

If you do not pay attention to numbers, whether you are broke, well off, or mega-rich, this will erode everything you have worked hard to build; eventually you will be left with nothing.

You can't gain control of your freedom if you keep interest rates, merchandise prices, gas prices, company expenses, payroll, etc., in a Pandora's box that you never open. You have to not only open it, you have to fully dive in and understand that box. Don't just say: well there is enough money coming in to pay for everything, so I am doing OK. That OK could be quicksand that you are sinking in, without even knowing it.

If you need help, hire someone or get a friend or family member to teach you. Not learning basic math is ***not*** an option. Go to a night class if you can't learn the basics of addition, subtraction, multiplication, and division. Hire a tutor. All you need is the basics to run your life and run a business.

Then apply your math to each item in Pandora's box, using one simple principal: get debt-free ASAP.

- Monthly debt payment? Can I pay more now and shorten the duration?
- Monthly expenses? Do I need five $5 Starbucks a week?
- Cable TV? Do I need that extra $40 per month super premium channels-that-I-never-watch-anyway?
- Do my employees even use the kitchenette? Or will a coffee machine do?

Go line by line through your expenses. Take any savings and apply them to paying off your debt.

Mastering math makes you aware of possibilities and disasters that were silently sitting right in front of you.

✓ Math can lead to ending debt.

✓ Math ends foolish spending.

✓ Math can prevent a disastrous loss of financial control.

✓ Math exposes the truth—numbers don't lie.

✓ Math can build your confidence in making great decisions.

#29

TIM MARSHALL—NO WAY HE'LL MAKE IT!

Tim's starting his own company? He's a great salesperson but...

When I opened my own office equipment leasing company in January 2008, the market was crashing around us, banks weren't lending money, and no one wanted to provide pass-through equipment to a company with no history, no money, and no collateral.

My competitors snickered. Even my family was a little wide-eyed with surprise. I ended up in a back room with a $75 desk and a telephone. I hit the market using the principals I had taught myself, the very principals of this book—activity, an open mind, and open-minded words.

I worked hard, never allowing my open mind to drop down the sinkhole of others' doom-and-gloom perceptions. I practiced every moment with positive activity. I listened with a 100% open and positive mind. The positive activity was my practice, and my open mind allowed me to absorb what potential customers were saying, and to enter their reality not mine. Did their world care that I was eating crackers, sitting in a room with no windows, my elbows trying to stabilizing the wobbly desk? No. They cared about their own life and business. That was their vantage point. So, with my ceaseless activity, which was really practice, I learned to enter their vantage point. From there, I became one of the fastest growing independent businesses in the U.S, making the covers of magazines and business newspapers.

My practiced communication skills and open-minded ways saved me. I practiced and practiced the art of action and words. No advertising, no social media, just very well-trained employees and salespeople who were taught the same open- minded strategies that I am communicating to you.

When you open yourself up to genuinely caring about the needs of customers as opposed to asking *what can I get out of them,* success will follow.

My company started with one customer, and we ended up having thousands.

This success all started from making my first uncomfortable phone call, then using constant practice to fully understanding the power of an open mind. I started actions and never stopped. Over time I went from that timid person, told point blank that I was a failure and a poor communicator, to now speaking about success and communications in front of a thousand people.

The best advice I can give to you is that the **only thing that you have total control over in your life are your words and actions.** Practice this control continually.

Always try to look at the true evidence of situations—not the negative projections created by your internal fears. Practicing an open mind reduces obsessive thinking and opens yourself up to redirecting your negative thoughts. How many times do we get caught up in a thought that just takes us down a path of despair and uncontrolled resentment? Redirect your thoughts into something that takes you into actions that mirror your intentions.

"To live your greatest day, you have to know what your greatest day is." —Tim Marshall

You've dreamed about it, now go do it.

ABOUT THE AUTHOR

Tim S. Marshall was recognized by *Inc.* magazine for starting a company in one of the worst economic climates in American history, and building it into one of the fastest growing companies in the U.S. for four straight years in a row. He is acknowledged as one of the top global leaders and salespeople within his industry. He is the award-winning author of *"The Power Of Breaking Fear"* in addition to *"Sales: Be Yourself, Sell Anything," "No Limits: How To Be Free While Getting Rich (For Millennials & Other Brave Species)," "Entrepreneurship: You're In Charge," "Personal Growth: The Radical Journey To Empowerment,"* and *"Relationslips: How To Embrace The Thorn & The Rose."* He is recognized as being one of the up-and-coming top motivational speakers in the country.

CONNECT WITH US ON SOCIAL MEDIA!

Website: timsmarshall.com

Facebook: Tim S. Marshall

Instagram: @timsmarshallprinciples

Twitter: @Tim_S_Marshall

YouTube: Tim S. Marshall

LinkedIn: Tim S. Marshall

Email: info@timsmarshall.com

Lightning Source UK Ltd.
Milton Keynes UK
UKHW01f1812270718
326398UK00001B/37/P